D0153879

Conservatives in Court

THE UNIVERSITY OF TENNESSEE PRESS
KNOXVILLE

CONSERVATIVES IN COURT

LEE EPSTEIN

Publication of this book has been aided by a grant from the American Council of Learned Societies from funds provided by the Andrew W. Mellon Foundation.

Copyright © 1985 by The University of Tennessee Press / Knoxville.
All Rights Reserved. Manufactured in the United States of America.
Cloth: 1st printing, 1985.
Paper: 1st printing, 1988.

The paper in this book meets the guidelines for permanence and durability of the Committee on Production Guidelines for Book Longevity of the Council on Library Resources. Binding materials have been chosen for durability.

Figure 2.1, "Genealogy of Some Early Conservative Groups": From Clement E. Vose, *Constitutional Change: Amendment Politics and Supreme Court Litigation since 1900,* a Twentieth Century Fund Study, © 1972, Twentieth Century Fund, New York.

Library of Congress Cataloging in Publication Data

Epstein, Lee, 1958–
    Conservatives in Court.

    Bibliography: p.
    Includes index.
    1. Political questions and judicial power–United States. 2. United States. Supreme Court. 3. Judicial process–United States. 4. Law and politics. 5. Conservatism—United States. 6. Pressure groups—United States.
I. Title.
KF8748.E67 1985   347.73'26   84-15287
ISBN 0-87049-449-X (alk. paper)   347.30735
ISBN 0-87049-567-4 (pbk.: alk. paper)

⬛ CONTENTS

Figures

Tables

In memory of my grandmother, Harriet Buxbaum

 **ACKNOWLEDGMENTS**

During the course of researching and writing this book I received guidance from numerous individuals, who deserve special acknowledgment. First, I wish to express my appreciation to the members of the Department of Political Science at Emory University. At some point, each faculty member read and commented on drafts of this study. Special thanks are extended to Harvey E. Klehr and Thomas G. Walker, not only for reading several versions of the manuscript, but for the strong educational base with which they provided me. I also wish to thank Linda Boyte for her assistance in the preparation of the manuscript.

I also must express my thanks to the attorneys and other staff members of the interest groups. These individuals include: Bruce Cameron, Ernest Hueter, Willa Johnson, Thomas Marzen, Paul Mc-Common, Douglas McDowell, Raymond Momboisse, Daniel J. Popeo, and Laurie Wieder. Michael Horowitz also provided helpful insights. Without their cooperation, this book would not have been possible.

Several others also gave generously of their time. Stephen L. Wasby and Richard C. Cortner, two excellent scholars, read an earlier version of this study. They will see that many of their comments have been incorporated in the final product.

Clement E. Vose deserves a paragraph of his own in this section. Without a doubt, this book would not have been possible if not for the scholarly tradition he established. After all, he was the first to explore the world of interest group litigation. For that and his comments on several versions of this study, I will be forever grateful.

Mavis Bryant and Barbara Reitt also deserve special mention. Mavis was a constant source of encouragement, especially sensitive to the needs of this novice author. Bobbie used her considerable editorial gifts to transform an early version of the manuscript into a hopefully readable, lucid, book.

I also wish to thank my family for their support during the past few years. Jay Epstein, always the trooper, typed several chapters and understood my work hours. My parents, Ann and Ken Spole, my parents-in-law, Janice and David Epstein, and my grandfather, Martin Buxbaum, provided me with continued support and encouragement.

Finally, I especially wish to acknowledge the guidance, encouragement, and scholarly tradition provided to me by Karen O'Connor. She read every word of this study in all its various stages (including untyped). I am proud that I can finally present her with some tangible results for all her efforts.

Research for this project was partially funded by the Graduate School of Arts and Sciences, Emory University.

PREFACE

Conservatives' political activity has exploded in the 1970s and 1980s, drawing the attention of both scholars and the popular press to the electoral and legislative lobbying of such conservative organizations as the Moral Majority, the National Conservative Political Action Committee, and the Eagle Forum. But the use of the courts by conservatives has been largely overlooked. Even the relatively few studies of use by interest groups of the judicial process have focused on liberal groups. In fact, most studies have been limited to descriptions of just one, the National Association for the Advancement of Colored People, and its litigation in one area — race discrimination.

Despite their narrow focus, these studies have fostered the development of widely held assumptions about the nature of interest group use of the courts:

1. Interest groups often resort to litigation when they view their goals as unobtainable or difficult to achieve in other political forums.
2. Sponsorship rather than participation as amicus curiae is the preferred strategy of interest group litigators.
3. Money, government support, frequent and increasing use of the courts, expertise, intergroup support, and extra-legal publicity are resources interest groups need if they are to succeed in their litigation efforts.
4. Interest groups generally obtain their objectives through litigation.

This book investigates the validity of these assumptions for three kinds of conservative interest groups not previously examined: economic groups, social groups, and public interest law firms. These labels, reflecting the major motivations involved and types of issues litigated, have been used primarily to organize research and discussion. All the groups selected for study share one important quality, their conservatism.

Chapter One reviews the literature concerning interest group litigation; Chapter Two, the activities of selected conservative groups that resorted to the courts during the first half of the twentieth century. The next three chapters describe the more recent activities of conservative groups that depend heavily on the courts. Chapter Six formulates generalizations about the nature of interest group involvement in the judicial process.

With some modification, the assumptions listed above, describe well the litigation of past and present conservative groups. Like their liberal counterparts, conservatives have entered the judicial arena with increasing regularity to achieve their goals. As conservative groups in the new wave continue to enter the courts in large numbers, just as they have inundated the executive and legislative branches, their litigation campaigns have evolved from emotional exercises to professional, well-planned drives.

This finding has important implications for future study and observation of interest groups as well as for the judicial process. The courts are increasingly being asked to mediate competing group claims, rather than claims simply between two parties concerned with narrow, personal interests. Although the effect of any one group on the decision-making process of a given court may be minimal, by adjudicating claims between groups rather than parties, courts will play an ever-increasing role as policymakers in the political process.

Conservatives in Court

INTEREST GROUP LITIGATION

Pioneer Research

As with many fields of political science, the study of the judicial process has undergone several stages of development (see Goldman and Sarat, 1978:417–23; Pritchett, 1968). During the formative years of political science, most studies of the courts focused on the judiciary as an institution and on the product of its efforts — constitutional law. Supreme Court decision making was thought to be the product of purely legalistic factors, the principle of *stare decisis* being the most important.

In 1941, C. Herman Pritchett startled the school of public law with his seminal work "Divisions of Opinion Among Justices of the U.S. Supreme Court, 1939–1941," in which he underscored the effect "personal attitudes" may have on decision making. Although Pritchett's theory was ignored through the 1940s, it was revived as the behavioral approach gained momentum within the other subfields of political science. In fact, by the 1960s much research on the courts focused on behavioral explanations, almost totally ignoring doctrine. Among the most significant of these early exercises was Glendon Schubert's 1962 article "The 1960 Term of the Supreme Court," in which he used sophisticated methodology to probe judicial decision making.

As the subfield of judicial process has entered the 1980s, behavioral approaches predominate, but to a lesser extent. Scholars now understand that the legal and behavioral approaches are not mutually exclusive. In fact, a relatively old but recently rediscovered focus of inquiry is now receiving recognition. It is this line of inquiry — interest group litigation — upon which this study is grounded. In general, this view proclaims that interest groups regularly act as external pressures, bringing cases to court specifically to facilitate the promulgation of legal doctrine that may be useful to their cause.

While the utility of the interest group litigation approach in understanding legal development has been demonstrated, it is somewhat counterintuitive. Scholars, like the framers of the Constitution, tend to view the judiciary as impenetrable by outside forces. Clearly, interest groups cannot directly lobby the courts as they do legislatures, because the rules of the judicial game differ quite dramatically from the rules regnant in legislative corridors. Robert Woodward and Scott Armstrong, in *The Brethren*, draw a vivid example of this difference in their description of the horrified reactions of justices Hugo Black and William Brennan to a Washington lobbyist's attempt to talk to them directly about a case (1976:79–84). Groups do have important functions in the judicial process, but in ways that are structured by the norms of the judicial process. Groups seeking policy outcomes go into court because they perceive that legal doctrines, the products of judicial decision making, may be useful to their cause.

The notion that interest groups lobby the courts to affect judicial precedent is as old as political science, initially having been conceived of by the father of the discipline, Arthur Bentley. Writing in 1908, Bentley was the first social scientist to comment on interest groups' use of the courts. Though he provided no direct evidence of interest group representation in the judicial arena, he did say that the justices of the U.S. Supreme Court were "a functioning part" of government that was "responsive" to group pressures and "representative" of all sorts of pressures, and that the justices used "representative judgment to bring pressures to balance" (1908: 393). He concluded not only that the Court, just like the other two branches of government, was susceptible to group pressures, but also that it mediated competing group interests (1908:388).

Not until 1951, however, were Bentley's ideas developed systematically, by David B. Truman. According to Truman, interests of all kinds would find it useful and even necessary to use the courts. Truman's examples drew heavily on the litigation of numerous business and employer associations, which is interesting given current scholarly focus on liberal groups. He discussed the associations' participation as amici curiae (friends of the court) in *United States v. Butler* (1936), a challenge to the Agricultural Adjustment Act, to illustrate the effect such briefs may have on the courts (1951:494–95). He also described the Edison Electric Institute's use of a test-case strategy to challenge New Deal legislation. Truman concluded that interest groups play a significant role in the courts.

Meanwhile, like many other political scientists who then were stressing pressure group activity, Clement E. Vose undertook a dissertation on interest groups in housing discrimination cases. His 1952 study, published several years later (1959) under the title *Caucasians Only*, demonstrated how the NAACP Legal Defense Fund developed and carried out a litigation strategy to persuade the Supreme Court that government enforcement of racially restrictive covenants was unconstitutional state action. NAACP litigation responded to that of white property owners, organized in St. Louis, Detroit, and the District of Columbia, who for three decades had persuaded local courts to enforce covenants that excluded blacks from their neighborhoods.

Vose also found that the NAACP used the judicial arena because it lacked access to other political forums. Just six years after its creation, in 1915, NAACP lawyers filed an amicus curiae brief, supporting the Justice Department's challenge to Oklahoma's "grandfather" clause that indirectly prohibited blacks from participating in elections (*Guinn v. United States* 1915). After succeeding in *Guinn* and several white primary cases in the 1920s (Vose, 1972), the NAACP realized that a systematic campaign in the courts on behalf of blacks could be important (Greenberg, 1977). This recognition, coupled with revisions in the Internal Revenue Code of 1939, conferring tax-exempt status on organizations that did not engage in "substantial political activity," led NAACP leaders to create a separate legal defense fund in 1939.[1] The Legal Defense Fund developed successful test-case strategies in three areas: education (see Greenberg, 1977; Kluger, 1976), voting (Greenberg, 1977), and housing (see Vose, 1959; Wasby, 1983). Test cases were initiated by the NAACP Legal Defense Fund because it was politically disadvantaged, lacking access to the executive and legislative branches of government, and sought redress through the courts.

Interest groups used the courts for other reasons, however. According to Vose's study of the National Consumers' League, organized by several women's associations in 1899 (see Goldmark, 1953;
Nathan, 1926), the league was one of the first groups to litigate systematically (see also O'Connor, 1980). It had been created in part
to lobby for laws to improve the conditions of women workers, but
once it succeeded it had to resort to litigation to protect the constitutionality of those laws when numerous employer associations
challenged protective legislation in the courts.

The National Consumers' League found itself in an unusually
difficult position. Unlike other groups that later used the courts (see
Truman, 1951:494), the league did not challenge the constitutionality of state or federal laws. Rather, it relied on state attorneys general to defend the laws that it had worked so hard to see enacted.
Realizing that such reliance would be problematic,[2] the league's general counsel, Louis Brandeis, and its leader, Florence Kelley, initiated a new tack: in *Muller v. Oregon* (1908), a challenge to the constitutionality of Oregon's ten-hour-maximum work law for women,
they sought to convince states to allow National Consumers' League
attorneys to litigate on behalf of such laws.

Brandeis's strategy in *Muller* was revolutionary for two reasons.
First, by insisting on sole control, Brandeis — on behalf of the National Consumers' League — pioneered a relatively new form of litigation for interest groups. Although the league's name did not appear on the brief and Brandeis did not accept any money for his
efforts, *Muller* is one of the first well-documented instances of group-
sponsored litigation. By insisting on controlling the litigation as a
condition for his involvement, Brandeis established a classic strategy, one now traditionally associated with the NAACP (see Belton,
1978; Westin, 1975) Second, after realizing that "there was little legal precedent upon which to base his defense of Oregon's maximum
hour legislation" (O'Connor, 1980:70), Brandeis asked National Consumers' League leaders to gather statistical information indicating
that long work days could harm women. The resulting so-called
Brandeis Brief established an important precedent: today interest
groups as well as private attorneys rely heavily on statistical, non-
legal information to buttress their arguments (see Levin and Moise,
1975; Rosen, 1972; Sanders et al., 1982). Vose's study of the National
Consumers' League provided useful information about its efforts

in the judicial forum, noting its establishment of classic strategies in court but also its fundamental stance: resorting to litigation when its legislative victories were challenged by employer associations.

Unlike the NAACP Legal Defense Fund in later years, the National Consumers' League turned to the courts to protect legislative victories, and not because it was disadvantaged in other political forums. Otherwise, the NAACP Legal Defense Fund's use of litigation resembled that of the Consumers' League. Both believed, for example, that control of litigation rather than participation as amicus curiae was critical to success. According to researchers, the National Consumers' League and the NAACP succeeded because they selected appropriate test cases. Moreover, both recruited skilled counsel; in fact, each was represented in court by men who later became United States Supreme Court justices.[3] Both also faced opposition from poorly organized conservative interests. In *Caucasians Only*, for example, Vose noted that white property owners' associations were unable to maintain segregated neighborhoods because the NAACP Legal Defense Fund was better organized and therefore prevailed in court.

Recent Studies:
Focus on Liberal Groups

Since 1908, then, scholars have recognized the usefulness of litigation to further *all* kinds of interests. Truman found that business and employer associations viewed litigation as an integral part of their lobbying activities, and Vose noted that liberal groups perceived the importance of organizing their litigation. More recent studies that build on earlier works, however, have focused only on well-organized liberal groups. Of the more than sixty papers, articles, and books on interest group litigation that followed publication of *Caucasians Only*, fifty-one investigate solely what their authors would call "liberal" groups.[4] Moreover, these studies, like those conducted by Vose, have tended to focus on highly salient areas of the law including race discrimination (Barker, 1967; Belton, 1978; Cortner, 1968; Greenberg, 1974, 1977; Hahn, 1973; Kellogg, 1967; Kluger, 1976; Meier and Rudwick, 1976; Meltsner, 1973; Miller, 1966;

Murphy, 1959; O'Connor and Epstein, 1982b; Osborne, 1963; Shattuck and Norgren, 1979; Shields and Spector, 1972; Stewart and Heck, 1982; Wasby, 1983), religious freedom (Katz, 1967; Manwaring, 1962; Maslow, 1961; Morgan, 1968; Pfeffer, 1981; Sorauf, 1976; Tenofsky, 1980), and sex discrimination (Berger, 1979; Greenwald, 1978; Cowan, 1976; O'Connor, 1980; O'Connor and Epstein, 1983b).[5]

Scholarly interest in liberal litigation in highly salient areas of the law is readily explained. First (excepting only issues of criminal justice), race and sex discrimination, union activities, and religious freedom are the issues that attracted the interest groups most often. For example, a longitudinal study of interest groups' participation as amicus curiae revealed that they participated in 53.4 percent of the noncommercial cases decided by the Supreme Court between 1970 and 1980 (O'Connor and Epstein, 1982a). As table 1-1 reveals, however, that participation was skewed and, in fact, generally correlated with scholarly investigation of interest group litigation in particular areas of the law. The precedent established by early studies is another reason that scholars have focused on liberal groups. Im-

Table 1-1
Amicus Curiae Participation in Supreme Court Cases, 1970–80*

	with amicus		without amicus		total number of cases
		N=		N=	
Unions	87.2%	75	12.8%	11	86
Sex Discrimination	77.5	31	22.5	9	40
Race Discrimination	67.7	42	32.3	20	62
Free Press	66.7	16	33.3	8	24
Information Act	63.6	7	36.4	4	11
Church-State	62.9	22	37.1	13	35
State-Federal Employees	55.0	11	45.0	9	20
Military	52.9	9	47.1	8	17
Indigents	52.5	32	47.5	29	61
Obscenity	51.6	16	48.4	15	31
Conscientious Objectors	50.0	5	50.0	5	10
Elections	48.9	23	51.1	24	47
Free Speech	44.8	13	55.2	16	29
Criminal	36.8	120	63.2	206	326
Others	64.0	27	36.0	15	42
Total	53.4	449	46.6	392	841

Source: O'Connor and Epstein, 1982a:316.

mediately following publication of *Caucasians Only*, for example, several other analyses of the NAACP Legal Defense Fund's activities were conducted, including those by Robert Birkby and Walter Murphy (1964) and Lucius Barker (1967). These early studies set the tone for later analyses.

Not only have studies focused on similar groups and issues, they have investigated similar questions. Almost all have attempted to discover (1) why groups turn to litigation, (2) what strategies they use to lobby the court, (3) what resources they employ, and (4) whether they achieve their objectives in court. Analysis of the conclusions reached by scholars who have asked these questions reveals widespread agreement.

The Consensus of Recent Studies

MOTIVATION FOR LITIGATION

Many researchers asked why interest groups would prefer litigation over other, more traditional forms of lobbying. Vose found that the National Consumers' League used the courts to protect its legislative victories, but most scholars agree that groups resort to litigation because they are politically disadvantaged in traditional political forums, that is, they lack access to the legislative and executive branches of government. Richard C. Cortner was the first to enunciate this belief formally. He defined politically disadvantaged groups as those that "are highly dependent upon the judicial process as a means of pursuing their policy interests, usually because they are temporarily, or even permanently, disadvantaged in terms of their abilities to attain successfully their goals in the electoral process, within the elected political institutions or in the bureaucracy. If they are to succeed at all in the pursuit of their goals they are almost compelled to resort to litigation" (1968:287).

Subsequent analyses reinforced Cortner's observations that the judiciary is receptive to politically disadvantaged groups. Frank Sorauf (1976) claimed that a coalition of groups opposed to the intermingling of church and state took to the courts in the 1940s after several state legislatures passed "accommodationist" legislation. Karen O'Connor (1980) found that women's rights groups often bring

test cases to court after recognizing that their goals would be unobtainable otherwise.

Cortner, O'Connor, Sorauf, and others (see Barker, 1967; Berry,
1977; Greenberg, 1974, 1977; Jacob, 1978; Manwaring, 1962; Peltason, 1955; Truman, 1951) viewed litigation either as a strategy to
be used when all else fails or as a technique to be employed when
goals are clearly unattainable in other political forums. Clearly, the
consensus among researchers is that interest groups resort to litigation when they view themselves as politically disadvantaged.

STRATEGIES FOR LITIGATION

Many scholars have examined the strategies interest groups adopt
to lobby the courts. Most analysts focus on two common, direct types
of group participation: sponsorship of cases and participation as
amicus curiae. Sponsorship entails legal representation of a plaintiff, preferably from the trial court level. Participation as an amicus curiae is much more limited. As amici curiae, interest groups
take part in cases simply by submitting supporting briefs, generally
when cases reach the U.S. Supreme Court.

Analysts widely agree that interest groups prefer to sponsor cases
from the trial court level. The control inherent in sponsorship allows groups to select the most appropriate cases to bring to court
and to develop a good record for later appeal. The National Consumers' League litigation provides an excellent illustration of the
importance of control. By representing states on behalf of the Consumers' League, Louis Brandeis was able to present the Court with
important information that otherwise would have been unavailable.
But perhaps the best examples of the importance of sponsorship come
from the NAACP's use of the courts. Several scholars as well as NAACP
attorneys have credited the NAACP Legal Defense Fund's victory in
Brown v. Board of Education (1954) to its use of a test-case strategy
and to its introduction of important evidence of the effects of
segregation at the trial court level (see Greenberg, 1974; Hahn, 1973;
Kluger, 1976). Without the ability of NAACP Legal Defense Fund
attorneys to pick and choose the best cases to bring to trial, it has
been suggested, it would not have achieved its objectives in the Supreme Court.

The amicus curiae strategy does not allow groups to frame the issues before the court. Because groups that use this tactic generally file briefs in already docketed cases in which the trial court record has been established, they have no control over the course of litigation.[6] Thus, while some scholars have indicated that amicus curiae briefs may affect judicial opinions and, in fact, constitute definitive litigation strategies (see Hull, 1978; Krislov, 1963; O'Connor, 1980; Pfeffer, 1981), others believe that the amicus curiae is little more than a propaganda tool by which an organization can show support for its membership goals (see Cortner, 1968; Freund, 1949; Hakman, 1966, 1969; Vose, 1981; Wasby, 1983; Westin, 1975).[7]

Despite not being considered the most effective lobbying device, the amicus curiae, like direct sponsorship, has been the object of extensive scholarly analysis (see Jacob, 1978; Krislov, 1963; O'Connor, 1980; O'Connor and Epstein, 1982a; Peltason, 1955; Puro, 1971; Piper, 1967; Sorauf, 1976). In one of the first studies, Samuel Krislov traced the evolution of its use (1963). He learned that amicus curiae briefs were originally used to provide the justices with "neutral" information. In the first U.S. court case in which such a brief was filed, *Green v. Biddle* (1823), the Supreme Court permitted Henry Clay to participate as an amicus curiae because the justices suspected collusion between the major litigants. Krislov concluded, however, that "the amicus is no longer a neutral amorphous embodiment of justice, but an active participant in the interest group struggle" (1963:703). According to Krislov, the Court recognizes this role and often treats the amicus curiae "as a political litigant in future cases, as an ally of one of the parties, or as a representative of an interest not otherwise represented" (1963:704). Similarly, Steven Puro's (1971) longitudinal study of the amicus activity of several organizations, including the American Civil Liberties Union and the AFL-CIO, indicates that the interest groups themselves viewed this device as an important lobbying tool. Other, more historical accounts of the amicus curiae (see Angell, 1967; Beckwith and Sobernheim, 1948; Corey, 1959; Northwestern Comment, 1960) also present evidence of its use as an interest group strategy. Nevertheless, scholars often ignore this tactic, claiming that interest groups more effectively lobby the courts through test cases (see Cortner, 1968; Freund, 1949; Hakman, 1966, 1969; Vose, 1981; Westin, 1975). The consensus among researchers is that interest groups have preferred direct sponsorship over the use of the amicus curiae briefs.

RESOURCES FOR LITIGATION

Scholars have explored the means by which interest groups increase their success in court. Not only must they select which litigation strategies to use—sponsorship and amicus curiae—they must also prepare themselves for their appearance in court. Some are well enough organized to attempt to prime the courts, that is, to create a judicial environment receptive to their point of view.

Initial studies indicated that at least six resources are apparently critical to organization success. Several scholars recognized early on that the amount of money an organization allots to litigation can affect the selection of its strategy, the kinds of issues it is able to pursue, and its success (see Cortner, 1968:291; Vose, 1959:42). In his account of the NAACP Legal Defense Fund's success in employment discrimination cases, for example, Robert Belton (1978) noted that without the proper funds to litigate these costly cases, it would not have succeeded. Conversely, Joyce Gelb and Marian Lief Palley (1982) have indicated that the Women's Rights Project of the ACLU tends to avoid this area of the law because it lacks the monies necessary to litigate properly.

A second resource that groups attempt to cultivate is the support of the federal government. Several commentators have noted that the United States government, whether it participates as a direct sponsor or as an amicus curiae, is exceptionally successful (Krislov, 1963:704–5; Scigliano, 1971:182). Consequently, scholars have concluded groups find it useful to seek out its support (Cortner, 1968; Krislov, 1963; Vose, 1959).

A third means that organizations use to enhance their chances for success is to sustain their use of the courts over as long a period as possible—*longevity*. As several researchers have shown, continuous and increasing use of the courts allows an organization to pursue a test-case strategy by chipping away at (or building up) precedent over time. The NAACP Legal Defense Fund's victory in *Brown*, for example, is credited not only to its selection of this case but also to its having brought several other school segregation cases to the Court before 1954. Through increasing use of litigation the Legal Defense Fund whittled away at the "separate but equal precedent" (Kluger, 1976; Greenberg, 1977). In Marc Galanter's (1974) terminology, the Legal Defense Fund and other kinds of groups can become "repeat-players" and accrue the resultant benefits of such status including "advance intelligence," litigation expertise, and "credibility" (1974:98–103).

A fourth resource researchers have identified, one that is closely related to longevity, is an expert legal staff. Vose (1958), Sorauf (1976), Meltsner (1973), and Manwaring (1962), among others, have indicated that a group's recruitment of attorneys who are well versed in its legal interest and who are committed to its goals can be critical to its success. Such staff members allow a group to keep abreast of potential test cases, to monitor ongoing cases, and later to litigate those issues if the group desires.

Expert attorneys can also help organizations develop a fifth resource—extra-legal publicity. As Vose (1959) indicated, for example, NAACP Legal Defense Fund sympathizers inundated law reviews with articles presenting constitutional justification for their cause. This traditional form of extra-legal activity can foster a judiciary that will be receptive to particular arguments (see also Newland, 1959).

One last resource many interest groups depend on is the support they can gain through cooperation with like-minded groups. A classic example was presented by Sorauf in his study of religious establishment cases. He determined that cooperation among several organizations was a key factor in the Court's ultimate adoption of their arguments. Others, including Berger (1979), Handler (1978a), Kluger (1976), and Vose (1959), have also attributed the success of various groups to their cooperative approach.

It was not until 1980 that these interest group resources were examined systematically. In her study of the use of the courts by women's groups, O'Connor examined the relative importance of these and other resources on their attainment of their objectives. She concluded that the importance of each resource varied with a group's preferred litigation strategy. For example, the longevity of an organization was relatively important for groups that directly sponsored cases, but unimportant for those that pursued the amicus strategy. Even those groups that relied on the amicus curiae, however, needed certain resources. Attorney expertise may be critical for amicus curiae litigators if their briefs are to be well crafted, for instance.

Yet O'Connor's findings imply that for groups that opt for the control strategy, the presence of most if not all of the resources was critical for success (1980:145). The evidence accumulated in many studies and correlated by O'Connor clearly indicates that interest groups typically devote much attention to the development of certain resources prior to their appearance in court.

LITIGATION SUCCESS

The question of success is the concern of many analysts. Some have attempted to determine whether other groups have used the courts as successfully as the National Consumers' League, for example. In fact, there is good reason to conclude that interest groups are highly successful in the judicial forum (see Barker, 1967; Belton, 1978; Cortner, 1968, 1975, 1980; Greenberg, 1974, 1977; Handler, 1978; Manwaring, 1962; Maslow, 1955; Meltsner, 1973; Neier, 1979; Puro, 1971; Sorauf, 1976; Vose, 1959). David Manwaring's study of litigation by the Jehovah's Witnesses, for example, documents their success in convincing the Court to strike down the compulsory salute to the flag. Similarly, O'Connor noted that the Legal Defense Fund "has used the courts with far greater continued success than any other organization" (1980:14). Its victories in litigation concerning restrictive covenants, school desegregation, the death penalty, and employment discrimination indicate how groups can use the courts to obtain their objectives. These and many other case studies as well as empirical analyses of success rates indicate that interest groups enjoy a high rate of success in court (Baker and Asperger, 1982; O'Connor and Epstein, 1982b, 1983b; Puro, 1971).

The Rationale of This Study

Bentley's "notion" that interest groups lobby the judiciary has, over the past several decades, become an important field of research. Particularly since the publication of Vose's ground-breaking work, scholarly attention to interest group litigation has mushroomed. The studies that followed Vose's *Caucasians Only* have reached similar conclusions about the relationship between interest groups and the judiciary:

1. Interest groups often resort to litigation when they view their goals as unobtainable or difficult to achieve in other political forums.
2. Sponsorship is the preferred strategy of interest group litigators.
3. The resources interest groups need are money, government support, frequent and increasing use of the courts, expertise, extra-legal publicity, and intergroup support.
4. Interest groups generally obtain their objectives through litigation.

These assumptions, however, have been derived from studies of only one highly visible set of groups, those representing liberal interests. It is unclear whether these assumptions apply to the activities of conservative interest group litigators today. Given the minimal scholarly attention that conservative groups have received, an examination of their activities is critical to a full understanding of the use of the courts by *all* interest groups.

EARLY CONSERVATIVE INTEREST GROUP LITIGATION: 1900–1940

Focusing on well-publicized liberal groups' efforts in the judicial forum, scholars generally have overlooked the fact that conservative interest groups also resorted to the courts during the late nineteenth and early twentieth centuries. They assumed that conservatives' efforts, unlike the liberals', were transitory and therefore unworthy of examination. However, as figure 2-1 shows, in their preoccupation with liberal groups, scholars missed an important fact. Several well-organized conservative interest groups recognized the utility of planned litigation early on, even before the NAACP made use of the courts.

From the beginning, while most liberal groups centered their litigation on civil rights and civil liberties, conservative groups' concerns were more diverse. This study groups these latter concerns in three categories, examining conservative interest group litigation focusing on economic issues, on social issues, and on conservative public interest law. These categories reflect not only the kinds of litigation pursued by the conservative groups discussed but also the motivation propelling that participation.

The Sponsors of Economic Litigation

Of the interest groups litigating during the first half of the twentieth century, those whose litigation focused on economic issues—

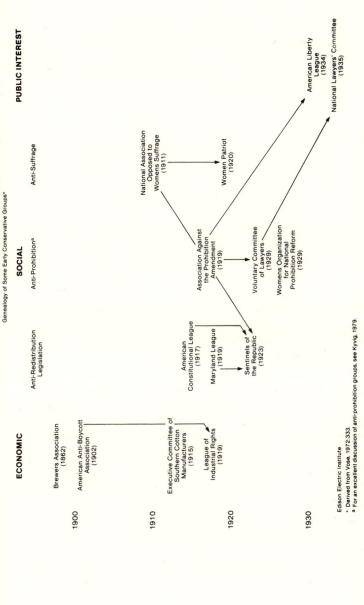

Figure 2.1

Genealogy of Some Early Conservative Groups*

ECONOMIC **SOCIAL** **PUBLIC INTEREST**

Anti-Redistribution
Legislation Anti-Prohibition[a] Anti-Suffrage

Brewers Association
(1862)

American Anti-Boycott
Association
(1902)

National Association
Opposed to
Womens Suffrage
(1911)

1910

American
Constitutional League
(1917)

Executive Committee of
Southern Cotton
Manufacturers
(1915)

Maryland League
(1919)

Association Against
the Prohibition
Amendment
(1919)

Women Patriot
(1920)

League of
Industrial Rights
(1919)

Sentinels of
the Republic
(1923)

1920

Voluntary Committee
of Lawyers
(1929)

Womens Organization
for National
Prohibition Reform
(1929)

American Liberty
League
(1934)

1930

National Lawyers' Committee
(1935)

Edison Electric Institute

* Derived from Vose, 1972:333.
a For an excellent discussion of anti-prohibition groups, see Kyvig, 1979.

From Clement E. Vose, *Constitutional Change: Amendment Politics and Supreme Court Litigation since 1900*, a Twentieth Century Fund Study, © 1972, Twentieth Century Fund, New York.

the American Anti-Boycott Association, the Executive Committee of Southern Cotton Manufacturers, and the Edison Electric Institute — were the most visible and aggressive. When they turned to the courts, they were reacting to prevailing historical circumstances that affected them financially. Their litigation during the first half of the twentieth century is, in fact, best understood in light of three phenomena: the rise of unions, the progressive era, and the New Deal.

OPPOSING THE UNIONS IN COURT

Both employers and employees began to organize as early as colonial times (Lieberman, 1950:2). It was not until the late 1800s, however, that either employer associations or unions began to flourish. With the increasing industrialization of the United States, workers felt the need to mobilize to combat poor working conditions and long hours. And according to Clarence Bonnett, "from the standpoint of the most efficient organization of his business, the employer need[ed] to consider the employers' association as indispensable, either for dealing with or for fighting the union" (1922:17–18). Many tactics used by unions certainly would have required a strong, organized response. During the late 1800s, for example, members of the newly formed American Federation of Labor (AFL) boycotted employers to force them to relent to their demands. Employers who refused to compromise were placed on an "unfair" or "don't patronize" list, which the AFL then published in its magazine, the *American Federationist* (Taylor, 1961:34).

This was the antagonistic climate that prevailed when the American Anti-Boycott Association was conceived in 1901. According to one of its founders, Walter Gordon Merritt, there was tremendous need for an organization "of employers to fight . . . union abuses and protect industrial liberty" (Merritt, 1970:4). But from the start the association was never thought to be a "typical" employer group. Rather, as Bonnett (1922:494) and others (see Merritt, 1970; Lieberman, 1950) have noted, the association was formed to act as "the" litigating arm of the major employer associations.

As described by Merritt (see also Wood, 1920:2), the association had humble origins. The initial idea for a special legal organization originated in a conversation among Charles H. Merritt, a hat manufacturer, his son, Walter, and Dietrich E. Loewe, a haber-dasher. All three were worried over the AFL's boycott activity and especially by its "don't patronize" list (Merritt, 1970:4). As a result of that conversation, "a meeting of the remaining champions of the open shop in the hatting industry" was held in February 1902 (Merritt, 1970:9). This group decided to invite employers who were being boycotted by the AFL to join a legal defense fund. Within the next few months numerous employers responded, but the majority were against the formation of such an association.

Even though most of the employers opposed the creation of an anti-union group, Merritt pursued his idea. To stimulate interest among other employers, he hired a Connecticut attorney, Daniel Davenport, to travel throughout the United States to seek support for an employers' association. Interest was sufficiently high to justify a call for an organizational meeting, he found. By the end of 1902 it was clear that Merritt's and Davenport's perseverance was rewarded: more than twenty-seven manufacturers representing twelve industries attended the meeting.

At this and subsequent meetings the employers agreed on two tactics. First, litigation would be useful in fighting union abuses. If the "liberties of men in industry" are "assailed" by "unlawful" union acts, the "protection of the courts should be invoked" (Merritt, 1970:12). This sentiment was further echoed in such slogans as "Organized violation of the law must be met with organized enforcement of the law."

In today's litigious society, the notion of going to court to achieve one's objectives seems commonplace, but the idea was not common at the turn of the century, particularly among employers. Few organized interests brought test cases to the courts; even fewer thought of lobbying the judiciary to achieve their goals. Most employer associations in fact avoided litigation, fearing adverse judicial decisions (Bonnett, 1922:555). Their forming an organization dedicated to the use of litigation, given such doubts, is all the more noteworthy.

The second point of agreement among members during the association's formative stage was that it would not formally commence its activities until it had obtained one hundred charter members. When this was accomplished, in mid-1903, a permanent governing board was established. A legal affairs department was also created, headed by Davenport and Merritt. The association recruited prominent attorneys, including James M. Beck, former assistant U.S. attorney general and future solicitor general under the administrations of William McKinley and Theodore Roosevelt (Keller, 1958:62). A public relations staff was also established to perform the exceedingly difficult task of increasing the organization's membership. Because prospective employer-members "were afraid that the union machinery would be turned against them" if they joined (Merritt, 1970:13), the public relations staff took special care to keep its membership list secret.

The association, however, soon generated the best possible publicity for itself: it won important precedent-setting cases for its employer-members. In two of its first efforts — *Loewe v. Lawlor* (1908, 1915), more commonly known as the Danbury Hatters Case, and *Gompers v. Bucks Stove* (1911) — the association secured major Supreme Court rulings.

Loewe involved a labor dispute between the hat shop of Dietrich Loewe, a founder of the association, and the United Hatters of North America. The union's leaders wanted Loewe to allow them to unionize his factory, a plan he adamantly opposed. After several futile meetings with Loewe, the union leaders declared a strike. According to one source, however, they were apparently unaware of Loewe's involvement with the association, which quickly "agreed to finance Loewe to the extent of $20,000" (Lieberman, 1950:57) to fight the Hatters. When union leaders realized that Loewe was prepared to fight, they immediately placed his shop on the AFL's "don't patronize" list.

The boycott put Loewe in serious financial trouble (Taylor, 1961:33), but the association "urged" him to fight because Merritt, Davenport, and Beck saw this as a perfect opportunity to test the legality of the AFL's use of the unfair list (Merritt, 1970:19–37; Lieberman, 1950:58). Beck and Davenport, in fact, had already developed a legal strategy for challenging the union's activity. They felt not only that the boycotting list constituted a violation of the Sherman Anti-Trust Act, but that individual workers could be held responsible for their union's activity. Because both Davenport and Beck were determined to win the case, the association and other employers promised to subsidize Loewe.

Financial support was critical; the case was in the courts for almost fourteen years. In fact, it moved up the federal judicial ladder

twice. First, the association had to secure a ruling that would sub-
stantiate its view that the Sherman Act was applicable to union activity. Although the association lost this point in a federal district
court, it later won in the Supreme Court. Once association attorneys had obtained a favorable ruling concerning the applicability
of the Sherman Act, they filed suit in a federal district court under
the act against 240 individual members of the Hatters' union to collect $240,000 in treble damages (Merritt, 1970:26). By this time,
however, the AFL had entered the litigation. It had filed an amicus
curiae brief in the first U.S. Supreme Court case. After the Court's
decision, it passed a resolution pledging moral and financial support to the Hatters (AFL, November 1908). The AFL followed up on
its promise by providing the Hatters with expert attorneys and financial support. As a result, when the case again reached the Supreme
Court for oral argument in December 1914, it represented a full-
blown interest group controversy.

The money and lawyers provided by the AFL, however, were unable to counter the association's early leverage and its establishment
of favorable precedent. Basing their decision on *Loewe I*, both the
district court and court of appeals ruled in favor of the association's
position. The union appealed, and in 1915 the U.S. Supreme Court
affirmed the lower court's judgment, ruling that "the circulation
of a list of 'unfair dealers' . . . is within the prohibition of the Sherman Act. It is intended to restrain and restraints commerce among
the states." The Court required union members to pay $252,130 in
damages.[1]

Although the Danbury Hatters case represented a "cause célèbre"
for the association, *Bucks Stove* was perhaps a more significant victory because of the parties involved. It was a confrontation of the
National Association of Manufacturers (NAM), as represented by the
association, and the AFL. It was a "real test of strength" for both
sides (Merritt, 1970:34).

The case originated in December 1906, when J.W. Van Cleave,
president of the Bucks Stove and Range Company and of the National Association of Manufacturers, asked the Anti-Boycott Association to provide him with legal representation. Because of local
union problems, the AFL had led a nationwide consumer boycott
against the company, causing Van Cleave some financial hardship
(see Taylor, 1961:34; Lieberman, 1950). Although association attor-

neys, including Merritt, Davenport, and Beck, were deeply involved
in the Hatter litigation, they gladly provided legal assistance to Van
Cleave. The association in fact viewed this as an opportunity to en-
large its constituency as well as to fight its arch-enemy the AFL, which
had promised to "make this a test case" (AFL, 1907:784).

In December 1907 Beck and Davenport secured an injunction
against the AFL's boycott (Keller, 1958:418). When union leaders ignored the court order on free speech grounds, they were held in contempt. Over the objections of association attorneys, the union, led
by AFL president Samuel Gompers, appealed to the Supreme Court
(see Merritt, 1970:38–47; Lieberman, 1940 for more detailed analyses). The Supreme Court opinion relied heavily on briefs presented
by Beck and Davenport in this and *Loewe I.* The justices dismissed
the contempt charges on procedural grounds, but they agreed that
the boycott constituted an illegal restraint of commerce.

The *Bucks Stove* and Danbury Hatters victories were significant
not only for their legal ramifications, but also for their importance
to the concept of group longevity. To be sure, the cases constituted
the association's first major efforts. But other factors may have been
yet more significant. First, association attorneys had selected ideal
cases for testing union boycott activity. According to the understand-
ably biased Merritt, "the unions could not have picked a worse case
upon which to state the issue. The employers could not have chosen
more wisely" (1970:23). Moreover, the association could afford to
pursue the litigation. Without the funds not only to bring the Hatter case but to support Loewe, the case would not have been decided. And finally, the association had recruited highly motivated,
expert attorneys. Davenport devised a brilliant legal strategy, while
Beck went on to serve as U.S. solicitor general and as a founding
member of the American Liberty League, an anti-New Deal group.

The cases did much more than set important precedents; they
gave the association the prestige needed to attract new members.
By the early 1910s, employers throughout the United States sought
the association's legal advice in fighting union activity. Interest
groups such as the National Association of Manufacturers (NAM)
and the American Newspaper Publishers Association came to rely
on the association to act as their litigating arm. In turn, by providing advice and expertise, the association soon developed a reputa-

tion as a "clearing house on all legal and constitutional phases of the labor problem" (Bonnett, 1922:449).

While cooperation with other employer associations was financially fruitful for the Anti-Boycott Association, this cooperation prompted unions to explore ways to end association activities on behalf of employers. On 14 January 1916, three members of the association were arrested for "having illegally practiced law as a voluntary association" (*New York Times*, 15 January 1916:7) after a complaint was filed by a labor union attorney. Although the charge eventually was dismissed as groundless, it illustrated growing union hostility in response to the association's threat to unionization.

Several similar adverse encounters with labor union leaders during the next three years apparently prompted the organization to change focus. In 1919, after an "almost unanimous" vote, its members decided to change its name to the League of Industrial Rights (Wood, 1920:2). Association members claimed that the name change only signaled its expansion into the field of industrial relations (see Wood, 1920:2, Merritt, 1970:96), but scholars have argued otherwise. James M. Beck's biographer, for example, claims that it indicated that the association would no longer apply the antitrust laws against labor unions. Instead, the newly named organization "concentrated its energies in the struggle to determine whether the law and the Constitution shall continue to function for the protection of the right-to-work and the right to conduct business" (Keller, 1958: 162). According to Keller, this new focus ultimately led to the league's demise. Although it continued to function as a legal advisor to several employer associations until 1940, litigation gave way to other activities. It lost its reputation as "the" legal representative of employer interests.

But the league's failure to achieve great success after 1919 is not attributable just to its changed focus. As Richard C. Cortner has pointed out, the "union-employee struggle" was not an isolated event; rather, it was part of "a broader conflict over constitutional doctrine and the proper role of the Supreme Court, itself in the government system." Thus, although the association's resources and attorneys' expertise help to explain its successful litigation, its victories were rooted in the Court's general acceptance of the laissez-faire doctrine. With the advent of the New Deal Court in the late 1930s, however, the league, like other anti-New Deal groups, realized that it had outlived its purpose and formally disbanded in 1940.

FIGHTING FEDERAL AID:
THE ANTI-PROGRESSIVES

Federal aid was another area of great concern to groups involved in economic litigation. Some, including the Maryland League for State Defense and the Sentinels of the Republic, presented legal challenges to federal aid legislation on the basis of moral or ethical opposition to such laws. Others, like the anti-progressive Executive Committee of Southern Cotton Manufacturers and the anti-New Deal Edison Electric Institute, opposed such legislation on economic grounds. Neither of these organizations was motivated by a social commitment; rather, they recognized the financial repercussions of such laws and so challenged them in court.

During the early 1900s many reformist groups including the National Consumers' League and the National Child Labor Committee attempted to secure state legislation that would protect employees from adverse working conditions. Relying on their powers reserved under the Tenth Amendment, states cited their "police powers" to justify passage of many pieces of progressive legislation during the early 1900s. By the 1910s, having succeeded in some states, progressives attempted to move into the national arena, lobbying Congress to enact progressive legislation under its commerce power. Their actions were met with tremendous opposition from various powerful employer groups.

One of the first manifestations of this struggle came in 1915, when Congress was considering the Federal Child Labor Act for the second time. This bill was designed to prohibit shipment in interstate commerce of factory products made by children under the age of fourteen or those made by children ranging in age from fourteen to sixteen who worked more than eight hours per day. It was supported by numerous reformist groups, including the National Child Labor Committee, the General Federation of Women's Clubs, and the National Consumers' League. But the progressives were confronted with strong, organized opposition. Represented by its executive counsel, James Emery, the National Association of Manufacturers, for example, argued that the bill posed a major "threat to industrial freedom" (Wood, 1968:52; see also Herring, 1929) and that it exceeded Congress's power under the commerce clause. Strong opposition was also voiced from a relatively new corner: the Executive Committee of Southern Cotton Manufacturers represented much the same view as NAM.[2]

Compared with the National Association of Manufacturers, which was established in 1895, the Executive Committee was a relatively new group. Consisting of "militant mill owners" (Wood, 1968: 49) the committee was organized in 1915 by David Clark, the editor of a North Carolina journal, *The Southern Textile Bulletin* (see also Vose, 1972:247). Clark organized the committee solely to counter "the movement to establish federal child labor legislation" (Wood, 1968:42). But in one of the committee's first attempts to achieve this objective it failed; in 1916 Congress passed the Federal Child Labor Act.

Clark immediately declared that his committee would challenge the constitutionality of the act in court (see Wood, 1968:80). Clark's suggestion of litigation, however, was not well accepted by other committee members. Their protests echoed those voiced by employer associations when Merritt first attempted to organize a legal defense fund; many felt that the courts would be a futile and perhaps dangerous forum.

But like Merritt and Loewe, Clark moved ahead with his plans for litigation without initial backing from the other manufacturers. He followed the association's course of action: he attempted to secure committed expert counsel. At first, Clark hired John S. Johnson, an attorney who had argued *United States v. E.C. Knight* (1895) before the Supreme Court (see Twiss, 1942:206–8). Johnson's philosophy and "connections"[3] made him a good choice, but he died shortly after Clark retained his services. However, Johnson did give Clark "advice" that contributed to the committee's ultimate success. He told Clark to pick an outstanding test case and to plot the course of the litigation carefully (Wood, 1968:93). With this in mind, Clark retained the services of O'Brien, Boardman, Parker,and Fox, a New York City law firm, one that not only held a laissez-faire philosophy but had successfully placed this argument before the Supreme Court in *United States v. American Tobacco Company* (1911).

After retaining this firm, the Executive Committee faced one remaining obstacle; it lacked the money to finance the type of litiga-

tion suggested by Johnson. To raise money Clark wrote letters to
textile mills "explaining the planned litigation" (Wood, 1968:86).
But like the association, Clark learned that the best publicity for
his cause would come only after he won a major case: *Hammer v.
Dagenhart* (1918).[4]

Hammer is a perfect example of organizational use of the courts.
The litigation proceeded through several well-planned stages. Even
prior to the selection of *Hammer* as a test case, Clark met with his
attorneys to decide when such a case should be brought and in which
court. Only after making these decisions did the group attempt to
pick the "right" case. To accomplish this, Clark toured the area
within the jurisdiction of the district court that they had selected
"in search of the perfect combination of factors" (Wood, 1968:92).
He found several potentially good choices; the group eventually selected from among these a suit against the Fidelity Manufacturing
Company.

The facts in this case, *Dagenhart v. Fidelity Manufacturing Company*, suited the needs of the Executive Committee well. Dagenhart and his two minor sons were employed by Fidelity, a cotton
mill in North Carolina. Under North Carolina law both of Dagenhart's sons were permitted to work up to eleven hours a day. Under
the Federal Child Labor Act, however, the older boy could work
only eight hours, while the younger could not work at all. Not only
were the facts as relating to the Dagenharts good, but Clark also
secured the cooperation of the factory in planning the litigation.
One month prior to the effective date of the act, the company posted
the new federal regulations on its door, and "explained" to the affected employees that they would be unable to continue to work.
A week later, having already secured the consent of the Dagenharts
and that of the factory, the committee's attorneys filed an injunction against the company and William C. Hammer, a U.S. attorney, to prevent enforcement of the law.

Within one month the district court (which Clark had carefully
selected) heard the arguments and ruled the act unconstitutional.
The judge never wrote an opinion, but when he handed down his
decision, he fully agreed with the committee's arguments, suggest-
ing that the federal government had usurped state power.

Once the district court stayed enforcement of the act, both the
U.S. Justice Department and the committee began to plan the strate-

gies they would employ before the U.S. Supreme Court. By this time *Hammer*, like the Danbury Hatters case, had become a full-blown contest between interest groups. The Child Labor Committee and other progressive groups expressed their support of the Justice Department. Once again the Court found itself mediating between competing group interests.

Unlike the association, however, the committee faced opposition from a tough opponent. Solicitor General John W. Davis, after some pressure from the newly formed U.S. Children's Bureau, agreed to argue the case personally on behalf of the United States (Wood, 1968:139). According to several sources, Davis was one of the great solicitors general (Frank, 1972:95; Vose, 1972), and his participation was considered critical. (Davis personally probably opposed the act, as evidenced by his later representation of conservative organizations in their attacks on New Deal legislation.)

But like the efforts of the AFL in Danbury Hatters, the efforts of the government in this case were negated by the leverage the committee commanded in initiating the litigation. Because it sponsored the case from the trial court level, the committee was able to win an impressive victory in the Supreme Court. Writing for the Court, Justice William R. Day accepted the group's argument and revealed the Court's acceptance of the laissez-faire doctrine: "The act in a two-fold sense is repugnant to the constitution. It not only transcends the authority delegated to Congress over commerce but also exerts a power as to a purely local matter to which federal authority does not extend" (247 U.S. at 276).

Like the association, the committee won a major case in its first try. And like the association, the committee pursued *Hammer* like an experienced litigator. Clark secured expert attorneys and carefully controlled the course of the litigation. This, coupled with the Supreme Court's predisposition toward a laissez-faire doctrine, helped the committee win an extremely important victory.

Again reminiscent of the association's ability to force unions to adopt other strategies after winning *Loewe*, the committee made enough of an impact with *Hammer* to push progressives into seeking passage of an amendment to the constitution regulating child labor. The committee played only a minor role in combatting this new effort, but other, more socially oriented groups took over where the committee left off.[5]

FIGHTING FEDERAL AID: ANTI-NEW DEALERS

During the early 1900s progressives successfully lobbied the state legislatures and Congress, but opposing groups including the Executive Committee of Southern Cotton Manufacturers convinced the Supreme Court to strike down much of this legislation. The progressive era had come to an abrupt end in the aftermath of World War I. In 1920, apparently tired of big government, Americans elected Warren G. Harding, who ran on "a return to normalcy" ticket, to the presidency.

Within nine years, however, the United States was faced with a mammoth economic crisis. Although President Herbert Hoover attempted to bring a halt to the depression, his policies had little effect. Americans overwhelmingly elected Franklin Delano Roosevelt president in 1932, responding to his promise of a New Deal. During the first one hundred days of his administration Roosevelt lived up to his promise, recommending many pieces of legislation to deal with the depression. Many of his proposals built on measures enacted during the progressive era.

While many applauded Roosevelt's efforts to cope with the financial crisis, opposition to his legislation came from several fronts. Some patriotic groups deemed it "un-American"; others, including the American Liberty League, condemned it as unconstitutional. At least one group — the Edison Electric Institute — challenged the legality of several pieces of legislation because of their economic ramifications. The institute realized that many of Roosevelt's laws, including the one creating the Tennessee Valley Authority (TVA) would financially destroy many of its constituents. It took to the courts when its efforts to prevent passage of that New Deal legislation failed.

Unlike the Anti-Boycott Association or the Executive Committee, however, the institute was not a legal defense fund, nor did it make immediate use of the courts. The institute was formed in January 1933 to replace the National Electric Light Association (NELA),[6] with the purpose of "purging the industry of evils that have grown up in some companies, such as looting of operating companies by holding companies, the publication of inaccurate and obscure financial statements and the use of questionable propaganda and lobbying methods" (New York Times, 13 January 1933:1). To secure its goal, the institute initiated a strict "code of business principles" for its members and gave its officers the right to discharge members who violated the code (*Business Week*, 25 January 1933:12).

Within one year of the announcement of the formation of the institute and its declared intention of "cleaning up" the industry, its constituents began to feel the threat of New Deal legislation. In particular, the industry's concern over the creation of the TVA led the institute to initiate a court test of its constitutionality. Created to provide employment and inexpensive power, the TVA was perceived by the utility companies as an "illegitimate function of the federal government," and thus unconstitutional.

After "vigorously" lobbying against passage of the legislation creating the TVA (Truman, 1951:494), the institute decided to take matters into its own hands by recruiting two attorneys — James M. Beck, former solicitor general and former counsel for the Anti-Boycott Association, and Newton D. Baker, Wilson's secretary of defense — "to prepare a legal opinion on the TVA's constitutionality" (Keller, 1958:263–64). The institute's purpose in securing a legal opinion was clear: because of the adverse publicity that NELA had brought to the utility industry, the institute hoped to "incline public opinion in favor of its viewpoint before the *Ashwander* case reached the Supreme Court" (Keller, 1958:263; see also Twiss, 1942:240). In addition, it wrote a letter to Roosevelt requesting that he "cooperate with the power interests for an early Supreme Court decision on the validity of the TVA" (*New York Times*, 18 December 1934:1).

Unfortunately for the institute, both strategies backfired. On the day that Beck and Baker's commissioned opinion was made public, the Federal Trade Commission "issued a report on the private utility propaganda efforts in the field of education," which negated the impact of the institute's opinion (Keller, 1958:264). Even worse was the Federal Power Commission's response to the institute's appeal to Roosevelt for cooperation. The institute, the commission claimed, "now suggests that the government cast doubt upon the validity of its own legislation by joining with [it] in litigation to test the government's own powers. In all the history of the American government a parallel for such a proposal can not be found" (*New York Times*, 18 December 1934:1).

Although the political climate appeared unpromising for a court holding in its favor, the institute went ahead with its litigation. It optimistically believed that victory was imminent, in part because it had secured expert counsel, including Beck and American Liberty League member Fordney Johnson.

But the institute's optimism was misplaced. Not only was the climate unfavorable, its attorneys made a major tactical blunder. While Beck and Johnson argued that the entire act was unconstitutional, and "regarded the case as one to test the whole plan and policy" (Freund, 1949:93), the government attempted to limit the issue to the facts of the specific case, which involved a contract into which the TVA had entered. On review, the Supreme Court fully ruled from the government's standpoint; it examined the constitutionality of the specific contract, rather than of the act. In fact, the Court claimed that:

> We limit our decision to the case before us, as we have defined it. The argument is earnestly presented that the government by virtue of its ownership of the dam and power plant . . . [is] a means of carrying on competitive commercial enterprise and thus drawing to the Federal government the conduct and management of business having no relation to the purposes for which the Federal government was established. *The picture is eloquently drawn but we deem it to be irrelevant to the issue here.* [Emphasis added, 297 U.S. at 339–40]

From the start, then, the institute committed major errors, and so never was as successful as the Anti-Boycott Association or the Executive Committee. Although the institute still exists, it rarely participates in litigation, except as an occasional friend of the court.

The failures of the institute can be explained in part by the Court's willingness after 1937 to uphold New Deal legislation, but other factors also clearly affected its performance. For example, even though it recruited skilled attorneys, the institute took no great pains to plan the course of the litigation. Nor did its attorneys devise new legal attacks; they simply recycled old laissez-faire arguments. Moreover, the institute clearly misread the government, as its attempt to coopt Roosevelt points up.

But perhaps most important, the institute was not created to litigate. Although it presented legal challenges to New Deal legislation, its purposes and responsibilities were much broader; winning in court, while important, was not its only or even its primary objective.

The Sponsors of Social Litigation

Groups involved in social litigation—the American Constitutional League, the Maryland League for State Defense, the Sentinels of the Republic, and the National Association Opposed to Women Suffrage—often supported the goals of their economic counterparts, although they generally did so on moral, religious, or social grounds and not on economic ones. Their fear that several pieces of legislation endangered the family led them to litigate in two distinct areas of the law: woman suffrage and federal aid legislation.

OPPOSING WOMAN SUFFRAGE

Although women activists called for suffrage as early as 1848, a strong anti-suffrage movement did not arise until the suffrage movement appeared to be gaining political clout. Thus, it was not until the turn of the century that those opposed to the suffrage amendment banded together to fight the increasing threat. During the early 1900s, several different types of organizations formed and eventually cooperated to forge a strong movement.

One of the stronger anti-suffrage groups to advocate the use of litigation was the National Association Opposed to Women Suffrage (NAOWS), which was later known as The Woman Patriot. Founded in 1911, NAOWS was composed almost exclusively of women who believed that suffrage would wreak havoc in the social structure. Interestingly, during the suffrage period NAOWS was not directly involved in litigation, though it did participate indirectly in planning the course of litigation. Its monthly newsletter, *Women Patriot*, for example, publicized the court actions brought by other anti-suffrage groups (see Vose, 1972:57–58), and when like-minded groups were considering test cases, members of NAOWS were consulted.

NAOWS played only a supporting role in anti-suffrage litigation, but the American Constitutional League (ACL) and the Maryland League for State Defense were major actors. The American Constitutional League was formed by attorney Everett P. Wheeler in December of 1917. Wheeler, who in 1912 established the Man Suffrage Association Opposed to Political Suffrage for Women, envisioned the proposed American Constitutional League as a patriotic states' rights organization dedicated to preserving the constitution. As part of that ideology, the ACL denounced the amendment because of its potentially disruptive effect on society.

Within a year of its formation the American Constitutional League was able to attract several important members because of its objectives and because of Wheeler's reputation. As a graduate of Harvard Law School and founder of the Bar Association of New York City, Wheeler recruited prominent attorneys including a future ACL president, Charles S. Fairchild, who had served as secretary of treasury under President Grover Cleveland, and attorney J. S. Eichelberger (*New York Times*, 5 January 1918:10).

The Maryland League was formed two years after the American Constitutional League by William Marbury, who had already created a lasting reputation for himself through his involvement in the companion case to *Guinn v. the United States*. In that landmark decision, Marbury unsuccessfully argued that Annapolis's grandfather clause was constitutional. Although he lost the grandfather clause case, his defense of the clause gained him a number of allies whom he recruited to the league.

Regardless of the prestige of their membership, however, these groups could only postpone, not ultimately halt, ratification of the suffrage amendment. Recognizing this even before ratification by the thirty-sixth state, members of the American Constitutional League began to consider alternative methods of challenging woman suffrage. After discussing the matter with constitutional expert I. Adriaans, who had helped Marbury in the grandfather clause case by filing an amicus curiae brief, American Constitutional League attorney Eichelberger concluded that a test case should be brought to court even prior to ratification by the final state. This view, however, met with mixed reactions from Marbury, to whom Eichelberger had sent a memorandum outlining his beliefs. Marbury believed that neither group should bring suit because of potential standing problems organizations could face in attempting to show the court that they are materially affected by the litigation, and that a nonratified state should initiate a test case instead (Vose, 1972).

The cases ultimately supported by the leagues combined both strategies. Two of the suits that reached the Supreme Court were brought in the name of individuals, but the American Constitutional League's case was initiated before ratification, while the Maryland League's was brought four months afterward. Because the American Constitutional League's case, *Fairchild v. Colby* (1922), was initiated prior to ratification, it generated more controversy than the Maryland League's *Leser v. Garnett* (1920). When *Fairchild* was first filed in a District of Columbia trial court on 7 July 1920 by the president of the American Constitutional League, members of the various suffrage organizations not only expressed their displeasure in public statement but were also permitted to intervene in the case (see *New York Times*, 22 September 1920:1).

Even without such opposition, the *Leser* case fared no better than *Fairchild*. While *Leser* was essentially the Maryland League's case, Marbury and Thomas Cadwalader (who was later instrumental in the founding of Sentinels for the Republic) were listed as counsel in both. Yet the combination of a well-planned legal strategy and expert attorneys was not enough to convince the Supreme Court to find against the Nineteenth Amendment. The justices, in fact, ignored their arguments and instead adopted those presented by Solicitor General Beck, who had handled the Danbury Hatters case for the Anti-Boycott Association.

In sum, the anti-suffrage associations were unable to stop ratification and enforcement of an amendment that garnered a great deal of support through legislative and judicial lobbying. Unlike some economic groups, however, including the Edison Electric Institute or the Anti-Boycott Association, the anti-suffrage organizations continued to fight; their battle simply moved to the area of federal aid legislation.

BATTLING FEDERAL AID TO WOMEN AND CHILDREN

Like their economic counterparts, socially oriented groups battled both progressive and New Deal legislation. Their desire to challenge such legislation emanated from a fear not of the laws' economic impact, but of their effect on social institutions. Their greatest crusades were launched against the Sheppard-Towner Maternity Act during the progressive era and against the child labor amendment during the New Deal era.

During the struggle over suffrage, both sides became experienced

coalition builders, learning how to cooperate to achieve their objectives. Even those organizations that lost their crusade against the
amendment gained expertise. As Vose has noted, "After all, the opposition to woman suffrage held off the likes of Susan B. Anthony,
Lucy Stone, Elizabeth Cady Stanton, Carrie Chapman Catt, and
their national organizations for fifty years" (1972:264). Soon after
suffrage was won, however, many former suffragists used their newly
learned political skills to lobby for passage of the Sheppard-Towner
Maternity Act, which provided federal maternity aid to the states
to fund programs designed to lower infant mortality rates.[7] Passed
by the U.S. Congress just one year after the Nineteenth Amendment
was ratified, its legality was immediately challenged by several conservative groups that viewed it as a major government attack on
the family. Groups including the American Constitutional League,
NAOWS (renamed The Woman Patriot in 1920), and the Maryland
League learned from the Southern Cotton Manufacturers' crusade
against child labor laws that passage of legislation represented not
the end of the fight, but only the beginning. Consequently, these
groups viewed litigation as the only method by which to challenge
the Sheppard-Towner Maternity Act.

These anti-progressive organizations were soon joined by another
ally. One year after passage of the maternity act and, in fact, as
a direct result of the law (Vose, 1972:265), the Sentinels of the Republic was incorporated in Massachusetts. The Sentinels, created
"by a few persons meeting at the home of Charles S. Fairchild" (Vose,
1972:265), quickly established itself as a prestigious group. Its
members included Louis A. Coolidge, assistant secretary of treasury during the Roosevelt and Taft administrations, who became
its first president; Alexander Lincoln, assistant attorney general of
Massachusetts, its future president; and Henry St. George Tucker,
a member of Congress from Virginia (*New York Times*, 1 December 1924:2; Vose 1972:265). The general objectives and the membership of the Sentinels complemented other anti-progressive associations. All these groups viewed litigation through test cases as the
only way to challenge the law.

Together, the groups decided to bring two consitutional tests of
the act to court. Their experiences with the Nineteenth Amendment
had shown them that they faced a difficult task and they therefore
wanted to present the Court with alternatives. The first case, *Massa-*

chusetts v. Mellon (1923), was brought on behalf of Massachusetts by Assistant Attorney General Lincoln and Attorney General Jay R. Baker but it represented "the spirit" of the Sentinels (Vose, 1972: 265). The attorneys, who brought the case directly to the Supreme Court under its original jurisdiction, claimed that the act violated the Tenth Amendment because Congress usurped rights reserved to the states.

The other case, *Frothingham v. Mellon* (1923), provided a much more direct example of interest group involvement in litigation. *Frothingham* was sponsored by several attorneys from Marbury's Baltimore law firm, including George Frick, who was listed as counsel in *Leser.* They decided that Harriet Frothingham of The Woman Patriot would be an ideal plaintiff. Frothingham was not receiving Sheppard-Towner Maternity Act aid; she was simply a taxpayer who complained that a portion of her federal tax dollars paid for the program. The Baltimore attorneys stressed not only that the act was unconstitutional but that:

> It has been held with practical uniformity by the Courts of the various states that a taxpayer has a sufficient interest to entitle him to maintain a suit against a public officer for the purpose of enjoining an unautho-rized payment of funds. . . . The appellant [in this case] maintains . . . [that] if these payments are made [she] will suffer a direct injury in that she will be subjected to taxation to pay her proportionate part of such unauthorized payments. She, therefore, has interest sufficient . . . to maintain a proceeding to enjoin the making of these payments. Her relation to these funds is exactly that of a *cestui que trust* to funds held by his trustee. Her injury would be irreparable because it cannot be calculated. She can resort only to equity to maintain her right. [Brief on Behalf of Appellant, October 1922:5, 10]

This argument was supported by several amicus curiae briefs, in-cluding those filed by American Constitutional League founder Everett Wheeler and Sentinel member Henry St. George Tucker.

Groups supporting the Sheppard-Towner Maternity Act lined up on the other side. Through the persuasion of Florence Kelley, who had lobbied for passage of the act, numerous amicus curiae briefs were filed against Frothingham (see Vose, 1972:268–69). Support through amicus curiae was critical, according to Kelley, because she thought Solicitor General Beck's defense of the act would be weak. Beck himself later admitted that he "was not in sympathy with the law" and that the brief was "largely prepared by the proponents of the Maternity [Children's] Bureau" (Keller, 1958:177). But Kelley's fears turned out to be groundless when Beck ably defended the government's position in the Supreme Court.

Beck's brief, coupled with public sympathy for the Sheppard-Towner Maternity Act, in part explains the Supreme Court's unanimous decision against Massachusetts and Frothingham in 1923. But interestingly, the Court never ruled on the act's constitutionality. Rather, it dealt with an issue Marbury had been concerned with during the suffrage litigation: standing. According to Justice George Sutherland, "The appellant in the second suit has no such interest in the subject-matter, nor is any such injury inflicted or threatened, as will enable her to sue" (262 U.S. at 480). The Court's decision in this case, which subsequently stood as a bar to federal taxpayer suits, remained good precedent until 1968, when exceptions were created in *Flast v. Cohen*.

Thus, although the Sheppard-Towner Maternity Act cases represented well-planned and creative challenges, they not only failed, but they revealed the potential dangers of litigation. When groups bring cases to court, the advantage inherent in obtaining a positive ruling — its almost permanent effect — can be quickly negated through the creation of long-lasting adverse precedents of the kind promulgated by the Court in *Frothingham*. Interest groups must therefore weigh the potentially positive impact of a favorable decision against the potentially disastrous effect of an adverse ruling before deciding to bring test cases to Court.

Not to be deterred by their failure in the Sheppard-Towner Maternity Act struggle, groups opposed to federal aid legislation soon set their sights on another progressive proposal, the child labor amendment. Like the Sheppard-Towner Maternity Act, the child labor amendment was backed by the National Child Labor Committee and several other groups, and with such support was approved by Congress in June 1924. This time, however, the anti-federal-aid groups were prepared to deal with opposition.

Opposition groups devised two strategies. First, both before and shortly after Congress proposed the amendment, the Sentinels held conferences to assess the effects of such an amendment upon the home and to devise strategies for stopping its passage. Attending the conferences were groups ranging from the American Constitutional League to the National Association of Manufacturers (*New York Times*, 9 December 1923:2). Second, anti-progressives recognized something they had not seen before: they could publicize precedents that supported their side. As a consequence of the efforts of the Southern Cotton Manufacturers, the Court had previously struck down child labor legislation. The groups could use this legal precedent as ammunition against the advisability of such a child labor amendment to the constitution.

These helped the broad-based coalition to stop quick passage of the amendment. But, as Vose has noted, interest in such an amendment was revived in 1933 with Roosevelt's inauguration (Vose, 1972: 250). Recognizing this renewed interest, the Sentinels moved quickly to reactivate the old coalition.

As interest in the child labor amendment grew through the lobbying efforts of the Child Labor Committee and other organizations, the Sentinels began to recognize the need for litigation. Two suits were launched in Kansas and Kentucky by private attorneys, who "were guided at every turn of their cases . . . by Alexander Lincoln," president of the Sentinels (Vose, 1972:251). Both cases, *Coleman v. Miller* (1939) and *Chandler v. Wise* (1939), questioned the procedures used by the Kansas and Kentucky state legislatures, respectively, in ratifying the amendment. Though both cases were decided against the interests of the Sentinels, they accomplished an important purpose: the litigation slowed down the lobbying efforts of the NCLC and other like-minded groups that were waiting for the outcomes of the court challenges (Vose, 1972:251).

The anti-progressive groups won the battle, but they lost the war (Vose, 1972:250). A child labor amendment never was ratified, but the groups lost both test cases, and in 1938 the Fair Labor Standards Act, which regulated child labor, was enacted.

Unlike the neophyte Southern Cotton Manufacturers or the Anti-Boycott Association, which were initially successful in court, groups opposed to suffrage and to federal aid legislation had been in existence for some time without tasting victory. Many of their attorneys were well-known litigators who had developed expertise in these particular areas of the law, and had gained repeat-player status as well. Other factors presumed to be critical to litigation success were also in place. For example, all the groups attempted to cooperate with one another both in their legal and in their extra-legal affairs. All received support at one time or another from government officials.

Yet these conservative litigators were unsuccessful in all their battles for the same reasons that some of their predecessors failed. First, they went for too much, too late. Rather than attempting to whittle down adverse precedent through a series of test cases, they brought massive challenges where there was little chance of victory. Second, like the Edison Electric Institute, they failed to recognize the changing legal tide and, in fact, did little to create a favorable climate. Thus, as Morton Keller so aptly titled his biography of James M. Beck (1958), their battles were often *In Defense of Yesterday*.

Conservative Public Interest Law

History shows that conservative groups involved in economic or social litigation have lobbied the courts. But at least one group, the National Lawyers' Committee of the American Liberty League, attempted to bring its version of the wider "public interest" to the courts. As indicated by several historical accounts (see Vose, 1958; Wolfskill, 1962; Rudolph, 1950), periodicals of the day, and its own publications, the committee believed that the public interest was best served when government avoided any needless entanglement with its constituents. Between 1935 and 1940 the National Lawyers' Committee specifically used litigation and other extra-judicial lobbying techniques to challenge all types of New Deal legislation.

Not only did the National Lawyers' Committee attempt to combine diverse areas of interest, it also represented the pinnacle of early conservative interest group litigation. The committee recruited the best conservative attorneys, many of whom had been involved in litigation conducted by the organizations discussed in the preceding pages. These attorneys were experts in particular areas of the law as well as in organizational litigation.

ESTABLISHMENT OF THE NATIONAL LAWYERS' COMMITTEE

The founding of the National Lawyers' Committee was intimately connected with the American Liberty League's activities. The Liberty League, an organization formed to oppose the New Deal, actually was an outgrowth of the movement to repeal the prohibition amendment. After repeal, there emerged a strong consensus among conservative leaders involved in repeal organizations, including the Association Against the Prohibition Amendment (AAPA), on the need for an organization to fight the New Deal (see Kyvig, 1979, and Wolfskill, 1962). This sentiment prompted Captain William H. Slayton, the founder of the AAPA, to correspond with Irénée and Pierre du Pont, who had financially supported the AAPA (Keller, 1958:257). When they expressed interest in such an organization, the Liberty League was officially formed by Jouett Shouse, who had been the last president of the AAPA, and by other repealers, including Irénée du Pont and Beck (see Wolfskill, 1962).[8]

Shouse's announcement of the Liberty League's founding created a wave of controversy. Shouse claimed that the Liberty League had immediately received "an avalanche of telegrams, letters and pledges of support" (*New York Times*, 29 August 1934:2), but some were quick to criticize the new group. Arthur Hays, general counsel of the American Civil Liberties Union, sent Liberty League leaders a questionnaire to determine their purpose. Others saw the league as an attempt to defeat Roosevelt in the 1936 presidential election. Almost everyone believed that the Liberty League would play an important role in the fate of the New Deal (*New York Times*, 29 August 1934:2).

Having just undergone the struggle for repeal, however, Shouse and the other members of the Liberty League knew they faced a difficult challenge. The United States was still in the midst of the Great Depression and Roosevelt was far more popular than prohibition had been. Given the arduous task ahead, the Liberty League leaders recognized the need to reinforce legislative lobbying with legal assistance. Thus, the National Lawyers' Committee was created in June 1935 to work with the Liberty League in meeting its objectives (Wolfskill, 1962).

The idea for such a committee actually dated back to September 1934, when Raoul Desverine, a member of the Liberty League and a New York attorney, suggested the idea to Shouse. But it was not until the following year that Shouse announced that a group of attorneys "had volunteered its services to the league" (Wolfskill, 1962: 71; Irons, 1982). This group of fifty to sixty attorneys, which formed the nucleus of the National Lawyers' Committee, was quite a formidable one. Desverine acted as chair, and other members included James Beck and John Davis, both former solicitors general and active organizational conservatives; Frederick R. Coudert, a well-known attorney; Joseph Ely, a former governor of Massachusetts; and several former U.S. senators and bar association presidents.

Given their overlapping membership, it is interesting to note that the only formal relationship between the two groups was not particularly important: the Liberty League was committed to printing and distributing National Lawyers' Committee reports (*New York Times*, 24 August 1934:3; Wolfskill, 1962:72). But more informal connections between the Liberty League and the National Lawyers' Committee were clear. As Wolfskill has indicated, members of the Liberty League, including Beck, Davis, and Coudert, were exceptionally active in the National Lawyers' Committee (1962:72). In 1935, Shouse himself referred to the committee as "the legal division of the Liberty League" (*New York Times*, 6 September 1935: 19). Thus, while the Liberty League tried to keep some distance from the National Lawyers' Committee, it was clear that the committee handled its legal work.

The NLC had the same general goals as the Liberty League, but it used different strategies for fighting the New Deal. Rather than employing more traditional forms of lobbying and propaganda, the NLC claimed that it would "consider whether any new law is within the power of the federal government" (National Lawyers' Committee, October 1935:3) and if necessary it would "contribute its services in test cases involving fundamental constitutional questions" (*New York Times*, 22 August 1935:1). This course was necessary because, as one conservative noted, "at the end of the 100 days . . . there is yet one hope and that is the Supreme Court" (Keller, 1958: 253).

ACTIVITIES OF THE NATIONAL
LAWYERS' COMMITTEE

Almost immediately upon its formation, the National Lawyers' Committee attempted to put its strategy to work. By August 1935, Desverine began to divide the group into subcommittees, each with responsibility for reviewing particular pieces of New Deal legislation (see Wolfskill, 1962; *New York Times*, 24 August 1935:3). The task of these subcommittees was "to pass upon the constitutionality of the various and sundry bills that were being introduced into Congress" (National Lawyers' Committee, November 1935).

Within one month of Desverine's assignments the first subcommittee filed its report. Chaired by Earl Reed, chief counsel for the Weirton Steel Company, the subcommittee on the National Labor Relations Act (NRLA) found that the act constituted a violation of due process and an illicit use of the commerce power. In its report, which bore a remarkable resemblance to a legal brief, the subcommittee concluded: "Considering the act in the light of our history, the established form of government, and the decisions of our highest Court, we have no hesitancy in concluding that it is unconstitutional and that it constitutes a complete departure from our constitutional and traditional theories of government" (National Lawyers' Committee, 1935:x–xi).

The report was unanimously approved both by the subcommittee and the NLC, but as one Liberty League member noted, "the ink had scarcely dried [on the report] before the league and its committee were attacked and bitterly criticized" (National Lawyers' Committee, November 1935). Attacks on the National Lawyers' Committee, in fact, came from all directions. Some claimed that Reed and the other subcommittee members were solely intent on pursuing the best interest of their own private clients, and were unconcerned with the validity of the legislation. Others, including Roosevelt's secretary of the interior, Harold Ickes, called the report "impertinence." Ickes referred to the NLC as "fifty-seven varieties of associate justices" (*New York Times*, 17 October 1935:6; see Wolfskill, 1962:73). In response to these criticisms, Beck claimed that the committee was not an elitist group and that in fact it would provide "free defense of the constitutional rights of any citizen unable to pay legal fees" (*New York Times*, 17 October 1935:6).

It was Beck's response to criticisms leveled at the NLC, however, rather than the actual report, that led to the committee's first major problem. In late October 1935, the Committee on Professional Ethics and Grievances of the American Bar Association (ABA) received a complaint charging that the NLC's offer of free legal advice was unethical. Although the committee never took the complaint seriously (see *New York Times*, 30 October 1935:44), there was, of course, some desire among National Lawyers' Committee members and the press to discover who filed the grievance. Joseph L. Kaplan, attorney for the National Support Roosevelt League, a pro-New Deal organization, immediately claimed responsibility for the ABA inquiry (*New York Times*, 1 November 1935:19). It was later discovered, however, that Atlanta lawyer and ABA member Carl N. Davie had brought the charge because he believed that the NLC's offer would encourage litigation (see *New York Times*, 18 November 1935:15, Wolfskill, 1962:76).

Whatever the grounds of the complaint, National Lawyers' Committee attorneys were seemingly justified in their lack of concern. In mid-November 1935 the ABA committee cleared the committee of any wrongdoing. In concluding its report, the committee stated: "All that they [committee attorneys] have offered is their experience and skill if and when any American citizen, however humble, is without means to defend his constitutional rights in a court of justice. The Committee is unable to see anything unethical or improper in such a course" (ABA, 1935:5).[9]

With this victory in hand, National Lawyers' Committee attorneys continued their examination of New Deal legislation and were prompt to keep their promise to challenge such legislation in court.[10] In fact, an interesting relationship began to develop between subcommittee reports and court litigation: in some instances, subcommittee chairs would file their reports, then use those arguments in litigation, which they would handle. The reports were usually written in the form of legal briefs, an expedient way of formulating legal arguments (Twiss, 1942:249). Also, by publicizing their reports prior to litigation, as did the Edison Institute, National Lawyers' Committee attorneys hoped to create a favorable judicial climate and thus maximize their chances of winning (Cortner, 1964:99).

One of the best examples of this strategy was the challenge to the NLRA, *National Labor Relations Board v. Jones & Laughlin Steel Company* (1937), and one of its companion cases, *Associated Press v. National Labor Relations Board* (1937). Shortly after the National Lawyers' Committee issued its reports on the NLRA, subcommittee chair Earl Reed filed suit on behalf of the Jones & Laughlin Steel Company. Simultaneously, John Davis, another National Lawyers' Committee member, filed on behalf of Associated Press. While these individual actions were purportedly brought by independent interests, as Benjamin Twiss has noted, "there was a close similarity between Reed's brief for the Lawyers' Committee, his brief in the *Jones & Laughlin* case and Davis's in *Associated Press*. . . . The briefs differed only in their application to specific sets of facts" (Twiss, 1942:249; see also Vose, 1958:25; Cortner, 1964:126–28).[11]

Though common among interest group strategies, the tactic backfired on the National Lawyers' Committee even before the cases got to the Supreme Court. It prompted a reaction like that caused by the Edison Institute's letter to Roosevelt; government officials became quite hostile to the league. In 1936, for example, NLRB members claimed that they were "three months behind in their cases" because numerous companies were using the National Lawyers' Committee's reports and briefs to support their arguments (*New York Times*, 15 April 1936:7; see also Cortner, 1964:98). This kind of reaction would have perhaps gone unnoticed had it not been for Senator Robert La Follette's Subcommittee on Education and Labor. Because of the publicity both the Liberty League and the committee had generated through the ABA Committee hearings and the issuance of the reports, the organizations had been criticized and attacked from all fronts. By the spring of 1936, however, the verbal attacks turned into serious charges of misconduct against Liberty League attorneys. At the La Follette hearings, for example, NLRB members and William Green, the president of the American Federation of Labor, linked Liberty League members to industrial espionage and other sundry crimes (*New York Times*, 15 April 1936:7).

While no formal charges resulted, the negative publicity generated by these hearings severely hurt the Liberty League, destroying the credibility its members had sought. The hearings alone were not responsible for the league's demise, however. After the reelection of Roosevelt in 1936 and the Supreme Court's decisions a year later in the National Labor Relations Act and other New Deal cases, the Liberty League realized that it would be unable to "repeal" the New Deal as it had prohibition. After 1937, members "nominated a skeleton organization to furnish reports on national affairs to industrial leaders" (*New York Times*, 24 September 1940:20), and by 1940 it formally closed its doors.

A variety of conservative groups have been an important presence in Supreme Court litigation since the early twentieth century.

The groups have been involved in economic and social litigation and have presented the courts with their view of the public interest. The efforts of conservative interest groups in court, however, did not end when the National Lawyers' Committee closed its doors in 1940. Conservative group involvement in economic, social, and public interest litigation has persisted. In fact, today it is enjoying tremendous growth.

CONSERVATIVE ECONOMIC
LITIGATION SINCE THE 1960s

At least three groups were involved in economic litigation during the first half of the twentieth century: the American Anti-Boycott Association, the Executive Committee of Southern Cotton Manufacturers, and the Edison Electric Institute. Although all three have either ceased to exist or have stopped mounting intensive litigation, other interest groups continue to represent economic concerns in court: the National Right to Work Legal Defense Foundation, the National Chamber Litigation Center, and the Equal Employment Advisory Council. Although the earlier groups have left the arena of the courts, they set precedents that have greatly affected the more recent groups succeeding them, as scrutiny of recent economic litigators reveals.

The National Right to Work
Legal Defense Foundation

Like the National Lawyers' Committee of the American Liberty League, the National Right to Work Legal Defense Foundation was created by the National Right to Work Committee to act as its legal arm. The establishment of the foundation in 1968 was intimately connected to the work and circumstances surrounding the creation of the National Right to Work Committee in 1955.

Passage in 1935 of the National Labor Relations Act, which had been bitterly opposed by the National Lawyers' Committee, served as a catalyst for the right-to-work movement.[1] A particularly offensive provision of the act, from the employer standpoint, was its authorization of security agreements between bona fide unions and employees. This statutory sanction of "closed shops," which required all employees of unionized companies to join unions, quickly became "the chief controversy in a large percentage of strikes" in the United States (Lieberman, 1950:332). Unions considered the closed shop imperative, believing their only leverage was in numbers. Closed-shop agreements also rid unions of the "free rider" problem, which gave nonmembers an opportunity to reap the benefits achieved by and for union members (see generally Pollitt, 1973:16–17). Employers, on the other hand, believed that closed shops represented an "encroachment on their natural rights" to deal freely with employees (Lieberman, 1950:330).

Shortly after passage of the National Labor Relations Act, employers found themselves at a severe disadvantage in their fight with compulsory unionism. During the late 1930s unions had garnered sympathy for their cause, while employers were objects of distrust. Recognizing that they were unlikely to convince the public that unions had encroached upon employers' rights, some employers began to claim that compulsory unionism denied workers their "right to work" by requiring them to join as a condition of their employment.

The right-to-work campaign caught on quickly, particularly after the hardships caused by several major strikes in the 1940s. Many began to believe that unions were controlling workers and not vice versa. Thus, amidst calls for curbs on union activity, by mid-1947 fourteen state legislatures had passed right-to-work laws that prohibited the denial of employment to nonunion members. During this period, Congress also passed the Taft-Hartley Act, which banned some forms of closed shops.

The state and federal laws were both only superficial victories for employers. By 1955 only one additional state had enacted right-to-work legislation; and more important, the Taft-Hartley Act, though adamantly opposed by unions, was from the employers' perspective limited in scope. Even after passage of the act, at least two other forms of union security agreements remained legal: the union shop, under which new employees were forced to join unions, and the agency shop, under which employees were not forced to join but were required to pay the union a fee. Thus, legal sanction of unionism in one form or another continued to prevail in the United States.

It was in this atmosphere that the National Right to Work Committee was formed in 1955 by Fred Hartley, cosponsor of the Taft-Hartley Act; Edwin Dillard, president of the Old Dominion Box Company of North Carolina; and "a few other Southern businessmen and some union dissidents" (Sklar, 1979:49), including S. D. (Duke) Cadwallader, a former railroad conductor (see Pollitt, 1973: 21; Crawford, 1980:28). Its purpose was twofold: to lobby more states to pass right-to-work laws and to eliminate the exceptions to the Taft-Hartley Act. From the beginning the committee made it clear that it was against compulsory unionism and not unions *per se*, even though most unions believed that to accomplish its goals, the committee would be forced to destroy the union movement.

Kansas was one of the first states that the newly organized committee targeted. The right-to-work campaign had been particularly successful in the Midwest and the committee founders believed that Kansas was a viable choice. At this time, however, the National Right to Work Committee, which described itself as "fledgling" (National Right to Work, 1979:19), could not have run a successful campaign on its own. In fact, it received much support from two prominent Kansans: Reed Larson and Louis Weiss. (Larson, who is currently the president of the National Right to Work Legal Defense Foundation and the committee, was president of the Kansas Jaycees, and Weiss, a prominent businessman, later served as the first chair of the foundation.) The efforts of the committee and of Weiss and Larson led to the state's adoption of a right-to-work law and at the same time helped to strengthen the group.

The National Right to Work Committee became so strong after the Kansas crusade that it began to pose a threat to unions, whose leaders perceived the committee as a union-buster group. Between 1959 and 1963 union pressure seemed to increase as the committee grew in numbers. During those years, there were numerous conflicts between the committee and the unions allied with government. Yet the more the unions complained to government officials that the committee was merely an "employer-front" organization, the larger its coffers and its membership grew. Increasing money and membership, however, did not help the committee to achieve its objectives. Because of the well-organized and well-financed lobbying of the unions, only three states passed right-to-work laws between 1955 and 1963.

Just as its legislative campaigns were unsuccessful, so too was the National Right to Work Committee's first involvement in litigation at the U.S. Supreme Court level. In 1956 it filed its first amicus curiae brief in *Railway Employees*, AFL v. *Hanson* (1956) (see Lewis, 1963:1).[2] In *Hanson*, the Supreme Court ruled against the committee's position, claiming that under the supremacy clause of the constitution (which proclaims that national law prevails over state law), a closed-shop agreement between a company and a union entered into pursuant to the provisions of the Railway Labor Act took precedence over a state right-to-work law. But in writing for the Court, Justice William Douglas withheld judgment on the validity of closed shops if other conditions such as union dues were imposed "as a cover for forcing ideological conformity."

In 1963, however, the Supreme Court favorably decided several major cases that were critical to National Right to Work Committee efforts. In the most important of these, the Court unanimously ruled that the Taft-Hartley Act left it to the states to decide whether unions could force employees to pay dues. Thus, state anti-security laws could be used to outlaw this practice. While the 1963 case did not address the use of union dues, it provided the states with some enforcement power over compulsory unionism.

The National Right to Work Committee did not participate in this litigation, but the outcomes of these cases impressed committee leaders, who now recognized the utility of litigation. National Right to Work Committee lobbying efforts in the state legislatures had not been particularly successful, leading some, including Larson, to believe that legislative lobbying should be supplemented by legal action. This perception, coupled with a barrage of requests for litigation assistance that the committee received after *Hanson* (Reed, 1982), led to the creation of the "independent," tax-exempt National Right to Work Legal Defense Foundation because "the Committee was not structured to undertake such large-scale legal assistance"(National Right to Work, 1979:4). The purpose of the foundation was to provide legal assistance "to employees victimized by compulsory union injustices" (National Right to Work, 1980:

5) and, in particular, to fight against the use of compulsory union dues for political activities.

Interestingly, its founders modeled the National Right to Work Legal Defense Foundation after the NAACP Legal Defense Fund (Reed, 1982; National Right to Work, 1979:4). In fact, their articles of incorporation are quite similar (de Toledano, 1974:1462), and like the Legal Defense Fund, the foundation immediately sought to recruit highly motivated personnel. Recruitment was facilitated because, like the Legal Defense Fund, the foundation had an available pool of talent from which to draw skilled personnel. Larson, for example, who was the "impetus behind the establishment of the foundation" (National Right to Work, 1979:17), simply moved from the committee to the foundation and eventually became its president. Similarly, Weiss became its first chair. Shortly thereafter the National Right to Work Legal Defense Foundation hired several people not formally affiliated with the National Right to Work Committee, including its current legal director, Rex Reed, who had been an attorney for both the Federal Power Commission and the National Labor Relations Board.

Having hired several committed staffers, the foundation was ready to launch its first court campaigns. Like the NAACP Legal Defense Fund, during its early years the National Right to Work Legal Defense Foundation worked actively to avoid "legal-aid-type" cases. Rather, the foundation attorneys attempted to select important test cases by which to secure their goals. In fact, according to the foundation, it has always "established as one of its major objectives the creation of new legal precedents which would benefit victims of compulsory unionism. While winning each case is, of course, critical for the rights of the plaintiffs involved, it is even *more* important in the long run to set new legal precedent in court" (National Right to Work, 1980:4).

Unlike the NAACP Legal Defense Fund, the National Right to Work Legal Defense Foundation did not face the difficulty of overcoming adverse precedent because of the 1963 decisions. But like NAACP Legal Defense Fund attorneys, those at the foundation realized that they could not litigate against all the manifestations of compulsory unionism. Consequently, the foundation carved out an area it considered particularly troublesome: union use of compulsory dues or agency fees for political purposes.[3] According to the foundation, "In no area of Foundation litigation is precedent-setting more important than in cases of union officials' spending of employees' compulsory dues for union favored political candidates and causes" (Legal Defense Foundation, 1980:4). Because the foundation, like the Anti-Boycott Association, was in a position to create, rather than to overcome, judicial precedents,[4] it took a decidedly different tack from that taken by the NAACP Legal Defense Fund. Rather than a single case-by-case approach, it sponsored several different, albeit well-planned, attacks, and filed amicus curiae briefs to establish a series of legal precedents against compulsory dues. Between 1970 and 1971 the National Right to Work Legal Defense Foundation initiated several suits, including *Abood v. Detroit Board of Education* (1977), *Ball v. City of Detroit* (1978), and *Seay v. McDonnell-Douglas Corporation* (1970). All three involved compulsory dues, but the first two dealt with employees in the public, not the private, sector.

Neither *Abood* nor *Ball* were fully developed until the late 1970s, but the foundation achieved an earlier victory in *Seay*. In *Seay*, National Right to Work Legal Defense Foundation attorneys represented twenty-eight nonunionized employees of the California plant of the McDonnell-Douglas Corporation, who had charged that their union, the International Association of Machinists, used their mandatory security dues for political purposes. In late 1970 a U.S. court of appeals adopted foundation arguments that security fees could be used only for collective bargaining purposes.[5]

Seay provided the foundation with a positive precedent upon which to expand. With this victory in hand, foundation attorneys immediately initiated numerous similar suits that relied on the *Seay* precedent. But in one of the first of these, *Reid v. United Auto Workers*, (1973) the foundation recognized that favorable precedent was often difficult to establish. *Reid* involved a dispute between nonunion employees and both their union and their employer—the United Auto Workers and the McDonnell-Douglas Corporation in Oklahoma. Reid and other employees claimed that the union and the corporation had entered into an agreement whereby all employees either had to be members of the union or pay agency fees equivalent to union dues. Reid objected to paying the fees, claiming that the union diverted a large part of the funds to political activities.

The facts in *Reid* differed little from those presented to the court in *Seay*, and National Right to Work attorneys relied heavily on the court of appeals' decision in *Seay*. But Oklahoma district court found little merit in this precedent and instead gave union officials the power to determine what refunds, if any, the petitioners deserved. The foundation immediately appealed, but a court of appeals merely reaffirmed the judgment of the lower court.

Because National Right to Work Legal Defense Foundation attorneys perceived the case as critical to their overall litigation plans, they sought a writ of certiorari to the U.S. Supreme Court. This attempt was a rather risky step for the young organization. In only one other instance had it participated in Supreme Court litigation and then as an amicus curiae on the losing side of another political contribution case — *Pipefitters Local Union v. United States* (1972). Given the foundation's lack of a repeat-player status and agreement among the lower courts, it was not surprising that the United States Supreme Court denied certiorari.

Foundation attorneys were disappointed by the adverse precedent established by the lower court in *Reid*, but realizing "that only new legal precedent would reverse this trend" (National Right to Work, 1980:4), they continued to initiate new cases. Rather than sponsoring mere copies of *Reid*, however, the foundation went on a new tack. Immediately after *Reid*, it launched a class-action suit involving more than two hundred Western Airlines employees, who objected not only to the use of union funds for political purposes but also to the principle established in *Reid*, which gave union officials power over fee rebates. The foundation's use of the class-action technique, which represented the first time it had been allowed in a union funding case, worked to its advantage: a district court ruled in *Ellis v. Brotherhood of Railway and Airline Clerks* (1976) that the union had illegally spent its compulsory fee and that its procedures for rebate were unconstitutional.

This ruling, coupled with *Seay*, provided the foundation attorney with enough ammunition to win two major cases in 1977 and 1978 — *Abood* and *Ball*, which had been pending since 1970 because of procedural complications. *Abood*, the National Right to Work Legal Defense Foundation's first case, varied significantly from *Reid* and *Seay*; it involved Detroit public school teachers who were forced to pay compulsory fees that they alleged were being spent for political purposes. Not only were National Right to Work attorneys dealing with public sector employees, they also were litigating in an "unfriendly" jurisdiction. According to one staff attorney, heavily unionized cities like Detroit are particularly difficult ones in which to win, but in this and other instances foundation attorneys were forced "to fight in the enemy territory" because this was where they saw the greatest union abuses (Cameron, 1982).

It was not surprising, then, that the National Right to Work Legal Defense Foundation lost *Abood* at the trial court level. After several years of further litigation and appeal, however, the foundation secured one of its first major victories in the U.S. Supreme Court. In 1977 the Court unanimously ruled on the *Abood* appeal that unions can use compulsory funds for collective bargaining purposes only.

> We do not hold that a union cannot constitutionally spend funds for the expression of political views, on behalf of political candidates, or toward the advancement of other ideological causes not germane to its duties as a collective-bargaining representative. Rather, the Constitution requires only that such expenditures be financed from charges, dues, or assessments paid by employees who do not object to advancing those ideas and who are not coerced into doing so against their will by the threat of loss of governmental employment.   [431 U.S. at 235–36]

The foundation's victory in *Abood* came as no surprise to the attorneys, who had long been involved in the litigation over compulsory fees. Since 1970 they had not only worked to build favorable precedent, but by 1977 had primed the Court for such a case through the submission of amicus curiae briefs and petitions for certiorari in numerous cases involving the fee and other compulsory union practices. Thus, by the time *Abood* reached the Court, National Right to Work attorneys were able to enhance their arguments by relying on favorable precedent that they had helped to create as well as to revive arguments with which the Court was already familiar.

Abood, however, represented not the end but the beginning of the foundation's crusade against improper use of compulsory public and private sector fees. The balance of this litigation, like that in prior cases, came in the form of sponsored cases rather than amicus curiae briefs. While the National Right to Work had acted as an amicus curiae before *Abood*, its attorneys generally view the amicus curiae as a poor strategy because it does not allow them to shape litigation. Particularly in this area of the law, they view development and control over the facts as critical. For example, in *Ball v. City of Detroit* (1978), another case that the group filed in 1970, the foundation won a victory similar to that obtained in *Abood*. Although Detroit was never considered an amenable jurisdiction, foundation attorneys relying on the *Abood* precedent were able to prove at the trial court level that a union was abusing employees' compulsory dues. In *Ball* the court ruled that city employees who objected to a union's use of funds for political purposes could have their fees kept in an escrow account until the union could prove that it would use the funds for bargaining purposes only. The precedent created in this case was later relied upon by foundation attorneys in another highly publicized case originating in Massachusetts, *School Committee of Greenfield v. Education Association* (1982).

But perhaps one of the most important aspects of *Abood* was that it gave National Right to Work Legal Defense Foundation attorneys a springboard from which to win a major private sector victory in *Beck v. Communications Workers of America* (1979). Initiated in 1976, *Beck* involved twenty telephone company employees who claimed that the Communications Workers of America (CWA) had misused compulsory dues. In August of 1980, a district court judge found that CWA had misused 81 percent of its compulsory funds, for political purposes. This first private sector victory since *Seay* was warmly welcomed by foundation attorneys. And not surprisingly, the foundation was at great pains to publicize its win, claiming, "The resounding success of the new legal precedents from *Seay* to *Beck* confirms the foundation's conviction that the establishment of such precedents is one of its most critical goals" (National Right to Work, 1980:7).

The National Right to Work Legal Defense Foundation's successful campaign against compulsory union practices was not without drawbacks. In fact, its successes caused the organization problems similar to those faced by the Anti-Boycott Association during the 1920s. As early as 1973, several private and public sector unions filed suit against the National Right to Work Committee and the foundation, charging that the foundation "acts as a conduit for 'interested employer[s]' to finance litigation against various labor unions" in violation of the Landrum-Griffin Act of 1959, which prohibits employers from financing employee suits against unions.

Like Anti-Boycott Association attorneys who had faced similar opposition, National Right to Work leaders were angered by this suit, believing not only that it was "designed to bleed [their] funds," to "destroy their legal program" (National Right to Work, 1981:2), and to "terrorize contributors" (Cameron, 1982), but that it also represented an act of revenge. And in fact, like the Anti-Boycott Association's opposition, many of the unions involved in the suit had fought against the organization in court. But unlike the Boycott Association's confrontation with unions, where charges were immediately dropped, at this writing this conflict still has not been settled. One of the major reasons this litigation has dragged on has been the foundation's unwillingness to disclose a list of its contributors. Foundation attorneys believe that "exposure would invite labor retaliation against the donors" (U.S. News, 1976:75) and that disclosure "would . . . intimidate people to stop giving" (Time, 1973:76).[6]

Such justifications for nondisclosure led some National Right to Work supporters (see de Toledano, 1974; Wall Street Journal, 30 December 1975:8) and attorneys (Reed, 1982) to draw parallels between this case and NAACP v. Alabama (1958), in which Alabama tried to force the NAACP to reveal its membership lists (for a full account of this case, see Osborne, 1963). While many unions perceive the National Right to Work to be an employer front organization and thus not to be covered by the NAACP precedent, foundation attorneys have used NAACP v. Alabama to support their position. In fact, they have even drawn analogies between the minority status of the NAACP's constituents (blacks) and National Right to Work's (nonunionized workers) to demonstrate that both would be "gravely impaired by disclosure of their names and amounts of contributions" (National Right to Work, October 1974:16–17).

Regardless of the judiciary's ultimate acceptance or rejection of this argument, the suit has taken its toll on the foundation. One foundation attorney estimated that through November 1982 the organization had "put in over $1 million," to say nothing of the value of the time lost by staff attorneys and leaders in giving testimony (Cameron, 1982). Moreover, the foundation was forced to divert

funds for additional security. When it moved to new headquarters
in 1980, it explained to its members: "The security of our office was
. . . a major consideration. The multi-union lawsuit . . . has shown
us the extent to which vengeful union officials will go on trying to
obtain the names of our contributors. We leave no stone unturned
in making sure this sensitive information is protected. With the cooperation of the builder, we have been able to incorporate into our
offices very secure facilities to protect our supporters' constitutional
rights" (National Right to Work, 1980:12).

Another serious result of the litigation was and continues to be
the National Right to Work's inability to muster support from other
groups. Although the organization cooperates with some conservative public interest law firms[7] and attends the monthly luncheons
held by the Heritage Foundation, a conservative think tank where
other conservative interest group litigators meet to discuss their
dockets, cooperation with other groups is "very rare" (Cameron,
1982). In several of their First Amendment cases, for example, foundation attorneys have even attempted to contact the American Civil
Liberties Union. But because of the foundation's reputation as a
union-buster, the ACLU "won't touch [them] with a ten-foot pole"
(Cameron, 1982).

Another indirect, yet serious, repercussion of the multiunion suit
was the attack of the Federal Election Commission (FEC) on the Right
to Work Committee's activities. In 1977 the Committee for an Effective Congress, a liberal Democratic lobby, filed a complaint with
the FEC, alleging that the committee had illegally solicited nonmembers for funds for campaign contributions. Subsequently, the
FEC filed suit against the committee in a district court.[8] After a hearing, the court ruled that the committee must refund the money to
its contributors and pay a $10,000 fine. While the D.C. Court of
Appeals reversed, in *FEC v. National Right to Work Committee*
(1982), the U.S. Supreme Court upheld the district court's decision.

Union actions have not only caused the National Right to Work
Legal Defense Foundation to divert funds away from litigation and
defend itself in court, they have also brought the organization under public scrutiny and may have affected its relations with other
groups.[9] The suit, however, has not affected the size of the foundation's membership or the size of its budget. According to one staff
member, very few have stopped contributing to the foundation since

initiation of the suit, and, in fact, as indicated in figure 3-1, its membership continued to grow even after the litigation was initiated.

At least some of this growth can be directly attributed to the success of its reliance on direct mail solicitation. Direct mail solicitation has long been a trademark of the National Right to Work Committee. In fact, some observers attribute its very existence to the pursuit of such a tactic (Viguerie, 1981:25; *U.S. News*, 1979:23). Leading force behind the New Right's use of the direct mail tactic, Richard Viguerie has not only provided the committee with assistance in this area but claims to be proud of helping the organization (see 1980:38). Some conservatives attribute the foundation's success in attracting members to the fact that it focuses on a single issue.

Thus, although the organization has faced some difficulties as a result of the multiunion suit, the National Right to Work Legal Defense Foundation appears to be thriving. In particular, staff members remain optimistic about litigation in their most successful area to date: political spending. They feel that they have not only carved out an especially important area, but are "absolutely changing the law" through planned litigation (Cameron, 1982).

The National Chamber Litigation Center

Unlike the National Right to Work Committee or the American Liberty League, which quickly established legal arms, the Chamber of Commerce of the United States of America waited sixty-five years before creating the National Chamber Litigation Center.

The Chamber of Commerce was created in 1912, but local chambers had been formed as early as 1768 (see Wennberg, 1951:19) and the idea for a national organization to represent commerce groups in governmental affairs was discussed as early as 1858 (Sturges, 1915:55). This idea first took concrete form in 1868, when the National Board of Trade was established in Boston, with all boards of trade and chambers of commerce "entitled to membership." When this organization failed to be wholly representative, the secretary of the newly created Department of Commerce and Labor suggested the need for a national organization to assist him in "fostering, promoting and developing of foreign and domestic commerce" (Sturges,

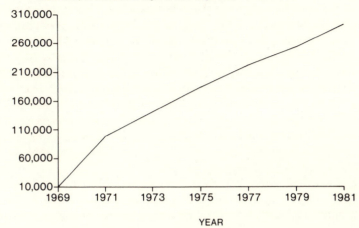

Figure 3-1

Membership of the National Right to Work Legal Defense Foundation*

* Source: NRW, 1981:14

1915:60). In response to this appeal, a National Council of Commerce was created in 1907, but like the Board of Trade it failed to draw serious interest. Three years later the Boston Chamber of Commerce tried to reorganize the board, but most believed that a new organization was needed. Because of widespread support and the genuine need for an effective body, in 1912 President William Howard Taft "Invited commercial organizations to attend a National Commerce Conference in Washington, D.C." to consider "creating a national body" (see Sturges, 1915:63). At this meeting, which was attended by 750 delegates, the Chamber of Commerce was founded, with the purpose of establishing "closer relations between commercial interests and federal officials and thus bringing about a mutual understanding" (Sturges, 1915:64; see also Childs, 1930:10–11; Rhett, 1917:47; Sibley, 1937:35–37).

Even though the Chamber was not specifically established to litigate, it has always recognized the importance of court decisions (Childs, 1930:245). Since the 1920s, for example, it has sporadically filed amicus curiae briefs in Supreme Court litigation. In addition, its general counsels have always supported litigation directly involving the Chamber. Like other employer and trade associations of the day, the Chamber was a member of the Anti-Boycott Association. Moreover, in 1928 it established a research department, which examined judicial decisions to keep Chamber officials abreast of important pending cases (see Childs, 1930:143).

But beyond sporadic participation as an amicus curiae and recognition of the potential ramifications of judicial opinions on business interests, U.S. Chamber officials did not aggressively pursue a court strategy until the early 1970s. Rather, during the preceding decades, they engaged in what they perceived to be a more effective form of pressure—traditional legislative lobbying (see Ornstein and Elder 1978; Zeigler and Peak, 1972).

While the Chamber continued to pursue traditional legislative lobbying, some conservative leaders began to recognize the absence of a business "presence" in the courts. Speaking at a Chamber luncheon, just one month before his Supreme Court nomination, Lewis Powell enunciated this view:

> American business and the enterprise system have been affected as much by the courts as by the executive and legislative branches of government.

Under our constitutional system, especially with an activist-minded Supreme Court, the judiciary may be the most important instrument for social, economic, and political change.

Other groups and organizations, recognizing this, have been far more astute in exploiting judicial action than American business. Perhaps the most active exploiters of the judicial system have been groups, ranging in political orientation from liberal to the far left. [Powell, 1971]

Powell's remarks seemed to spur the Chamber into action. Between 1972 and 1977 the Chamber's attorneys initiated a series of cases challenging certain types of employee practices, especially union activity. Like its predecessors, the Anti-Boycott Association and the National Right to Work Legal Defense Foundation, the Chamber believed that union demands placed undue financial hardship on business, and so it "aggressively" sought to counter those demands through a program of labor law litigation (McDowell, 1982).

The Chamber quickly learned that most such litigation was quite costly and complex. Standing, in particular, proved to be a major problem. Within five years of its decision to litigate on behalf of its membership, the Chamber "said enough of this" when it ran out of funds and when many of its challenges had been unsuccessful. Yet it clearly recognized the need for continued litigation on behalf of business because of the Supreme Court's recent involvement in issues including affirmative action and pregnancy disability benefits. That is why, in March of 1977, leaders of the Chamber formed the National Chamber Litigation Center as a nonprofit, tax-exempt membership organization, which would be the "only [firm] devoted exclusively to representation of business before the courts and regulatory agencies" (Gray, 1978:26; Wieder, 1982). In fact, because of the center's exclusive emphasis on "business," it is "chartered" under section 501(c)(6) of the Internal Revenue Code. Thus, contributions to the center can be deducted as business expenses rather than as charitable deductions.

The establishment and initial purposes of the National Chamber Litigation Center indicate that the Chamber recognized and attempted to rectify the problems incurred during its aggressive labor law program. Rather than funding the litigation program from its own budget, the center was to be totally funded by outside business, with the exception of $100,000 in seed money. In addition, because it was to be a membership-based organization, leaders of the Chamber thought that the center would be better equipped "to represent individual businesses," rather than simply to litigate on behalf of the Chamber. Thus, while the general counsel of the Chamber would continue to handle all the "routine" cases of the organization, the National Chamber Litigation Center was to be the "voice" for its business members (Wieder, 1982). Finally, to decrease litigation expenses and to become involved in a broader range of business cases, the center was to rely more heavily on the amicus curiae, rather than the sponsorship, strategy. As initially planned, therefore, the activities of the center were to be remarkably different from any others the Chamber had previously conducted.

The National Chamber Litigation Center has not strayed much from the blueprint of its founders. It officially opened its doors in March of 1977 with seed money from the Chamber and with two staff attorneys: litigation director Stanley Kaleczyc and senior labor counsel Stephen Bokat. But several companies quickly joined, and within three years the center had a thousand members and a budget of approximately $500,000 (Wieder, 1982; National Chamber Litigation Center, 1980–81:1). While these funds were insufficient to undertake the sort of aggressive litigation that the Chamber had earlier attempted, they provided the center with enough money to pursue the preferred strategy of its founders: participation as amicus curiae.

According to one staff member, the National Chamber Litigation Center has a "stringent" review process (see Gray, 1978) for selection of cases for submission of amicus curiae briefs. Most cases are initially selected from the *Federal Register* by staff attorneys, who look for those that have wide ramifications for business and that have realistic chances of winning. The center claims that a case "must meet four criteria" before it will enter: "It must involve an issue of national concern to business, there must be no one else representing the broad business perspective. . . . There must be a reasonable expectation of success and the issue must fit within NCLC's overall priorities and resources" (National Chamber Litigation Center, n.d.). Identified cases are then reviewed by internal center committees. The case selection process is highly formalized. Each case, in fact, is carefully scrutinized so that center participation will have some impact on the ultimate resolution of the litigation.

The utility of the amicus curiae tactic has been evident only in some National Chamber Litigation Center cases. In *First National Maintenance Corporation v.* NLRB (1981), for example, the center, in its amicus curiae brief filed on behalf of the Chamber, argued that business should not be forced to bargain with unions prior to terminating operations in a facility "when the company decision is based solely upon economic decisions" (National Chamber Litigation Center, fall 1981:3). In a 7-to-2 decision, without specifically mentioning the center's brief, the Supreme Court adopted its argument in full. The precedent established by the Court in this case led the NLRB to reverse a ruling in *Brockway Motor Truck v.* NLRB (1978), a similar case in which the center had participated. Thus, like the National Right to Work Legal Defense Foundation and several earlier economic groups, the center helped to build important precedent, but through the less expensive amicus route.

Actually, however, it would appear that much of its amicus curiae activity has been responsive to the demands of its members; the National Chamber Litigation Center files "on demand" amicus curiae briefs at the request of member companies. For example, in *Halliburton Services v. International Association of Machinists* (1982), a case involving the location of a union representation election, the center filed an amicus curiae brief after Halliburton claimed that the group's support would be critical because numerous unions had filed on the other side (Wieder, 1982). Although staffers at the center consider this "on demand" type of participation essential for the economic survival of the organization, it has inherent dangers. Rather than participating in cases that it believes to have significant ramifications, the center may resign itself to participating in trivial litigation or in cases it sees as "losers." By attempting to appease its membership, the organization may end up in a Catch-22 situation wherein it selects poor cases to attract members but fails to hold them because it is unable to win those cases.

Recently there has been evidence of subtle changes in the National Chamber Litigation Center's activities. This change is apparent in two ways. First, although the center has specifically stated that it will not enter cases in which the "business perspective is already being adequately presented," it has formed relationships with other like-minded organizations. Like the National Right to Work Legal Defense Foundation, for example, it attends the Heritage Foundation luncheons. At one luncheon, in fact, center attorneys were asked by another conservative group to file an amicus curiae brief in support of their position. Instead of participating, however, center lawyers contacted a conservative public interest law firm that they felt was better equipped to handle the case (Wieder, 1982). Center attorneys in some instances call a like-minded group, the Equal Employment Advisory Council, to find out if it is briefing a case. If so, the center stays out unless the case is very important. This philosophy of "non-cooperation" in litigation, while markedly different from the approach of most liberal groups, seems to be effective: it prevents needless duplication of effort and thus conserves valuable time and resources. But to follow this tactic, the center recognizes the importance of keeping abreast of other organizations' activities.

A second change that the National Chamber Litigation Center has made involves its choice of litigation strategies. Although it still considers the amicus curiae cost effective,[10] it has begun to sponsor more cases (Wieder, 1982), a strategy it has used only sporadically since its formation. In fact, the first case ever sponsored by the center, *Bread Political Action Committee v. Federal Election Commission* (1982), was not decided by the U.S. Supreme Court until 1982, although center attorneys initiated *Bread* within weeks of the group's creation. *Bread* involved a challenge to a provision of the Federal Election Campaign Act of 1971 (FECA) that "limited the extent to which [trade] associations and their PACs may solicit funds for political purposes." To challenge this restriction, the center represented three trade associations.

But like the obstacles encountered during its earlier aggressive litigation campaign, procedural problems also became a major issue for the National Chamber Litigation Center in *Bread*. Because FECA specified three types of plaintiffs who could invoke expedited review, in a unanimous opinion the U.S. Supreme Court held that trade associations were not entitled to such review. Writing for the Court, Justice Sandra Day O'Connor declared that "we cannot impute to Congress the intention to confer standing on the broadest class imaginable. We do not assume the maximum jurisdiction permitted by the Constitution, absent a clearer mandate from Congress" (71 at L. Ed. 2d at 438).

Thus, the National Chamber Litigation Center, in its first sponsored case, encountered problems similar to those experienced by the Chamber during the early 1970s. But regardless of the center's ability to overcome legal obstacles such as standing, its future as a sponsor, or even as an amicus curiae, may be further hampered. Although appearances before the Court may help the center gain repeat-player status, much will depend on its ability to obtain adequate funding and staff. Noting the recession, the center representatives admit that contributions decreased during 1982. Moreover, in late 1982 Kaleczyc resigned to return to private practice. Whether the center can adequately deal with these problems may determine its future as a viable litigating organization.

The Equal Employment Advisory Council

At the same time the Chamber was pursuing an aggressive and expensive litigation strategy prior to the creation of the National Chamber Litigation Center, a number of other attorneys and businesses unassociated with the Chamber became increasingly concerned about recent developments in employment discrimination law. For example, in 1976, the U.S. Supreme Court agreed to hear arguments in *Regents of the University of California v. Bakke* (1978) and in several other cases involving what employers viewed as costly affirmative action plans. Not only was the outcome of the affirmative action issue uncertain, but the incoming Carter administration seemed to be even more threatening to the business community. Many industries realized that the Carter administration, unlike preceding Republican administrations, would be hospitable to affirmative action plans. Business interests saw that government, coupled almost certainly with such well-respected liberal organizations such as the NAACP Legal Defense Fund, would present formidable opposition in court (McDowell, 1982).

Because they believed that employers were not well represented and were unnecessarily losing cases, several attorneys, including

members of the Washington, D.C.-based labor law firm of Mc-
Guiness and Williams, in conjunction with others whom they met
at bar association meetings, founded the Equal Employment Advisory Council (EEAC) in 1976.[11] Given their common experience as
labor law attorneys, founders of the EEAC were well aware of the
pitfalls of employment discrimination litigation. In particular, they
recognized that the Chamber had lost a great deal of money on unsuccessful litigation and that National Right to Work had spent
equally large sums on deciding whether to disclose its membership
lists (McDowell, 1982).

To avoid such problems, the founders of the EEAC agreed on three
tactics. First, rather than attempting to litigate in a broad range
of business issues, they would concentrate solely on monitoring federal equal employment opportunity litigation. Attorneys felt that
this would give the group a chance not only to establish a reputation in a particular area of the law but also help employers financially, as employment discrimination litigation was the most costly
area of litigation for them. Since its establishment the Equal Employment Advisory Council has not veered from this course. To date,
all of its court appearances have involved some aspect of employment discrimination. But as litigation in this area has become increasingly broad in focus, EEAC's case involvement has expanded.
For example, although it still participates in cases involving affirmative action, it also now regularly submits briefs in employment
discrimination litigation involving the certification of classes and
awards of attorneys' fees.

A second point of agreement among Equal Employment Advisory Council founders dealt with the selection of a litigation strategy. All concurred that Equal Employment Advisory Council should
"not become a party, whether as a plaintiff or . . . intervenor in
any litigation" (EEAC, 1982:1). Thus, unlike the National Chamber
Litigation Center, which was established primarily to file amicus
curiae briefs but now reveals a "trend" toward sponsorship (Wieder,
1982), the EEAC participates solely as an amicus curiae. The belief
of its founders in the utility of this strategy stemmed from several
considerations, the most important of which was its attorneys' belief that "except in rare instances" participation as amicus curiae
 has the same impact as direct sponsorship, but at a far lower cost

(EEAC, 1982:1; McDowell, 1982). Some of its attorneys, in fact, claim that the amicus curiae is actually more effective in this area of the law because they can "take a broader perspective" by "paring down other issues [they are] not interested in" (McDowell, 1982).

To facilitate the impact of its amicus curiae strategy, the Equal Employment Advisory Council's case selection committee, whose members are charged with selecting and briefing cases for participation, carefully reviews potential cases. Like the National Chamber Litigation Center, cases are identified either through attorney review of reported federal cases or through membership suggestions. At this stage in the screening process, committee members generally select cases that have proceeded at least to the court of appeals stage and that involve potentially "precedent setting" issues (EEAC, 1982:1–3). Once individual committee members identify these cases, all members either meet or "are polled for their recommendations" before the board of directors convenes for final consideration. At this last stage in the process, the board gives a great deal of consideration to the position of business generally. If it believes that a particular case is controversial — unrepresentative of the entire business community and not just of its own membership — it will not permit EEAC participation. Thus, while the EEAC is concerned about the views of its members, unlike the National Chamber Litigation Center it will not participate in cases simply to please its members. Rather, according to one staff attorney, "we do this [amicus curiae participation] for impact — not to get publicity. . . . We are not PR people, we're lawyers" (McDowell, 1982).

The Equal Employment Advisory Council's goal of legal impact rather than of publicity for the organization matches the third point of agreement among its founders; the EEAC has, until recently, tried to minimize public and media attention for fear of "retaliation by government and civil rights groups" like that experienced by National Right to Work (Bendeck, 1982:21; *Business Week*, 1980:100). The EEAC's initial desire to keep a low profile apparently helped it to attract supporters. Its membership rolls have grown every year. And although like other economic litigators discussed it will not disclose its membership, it claims to represent thirty-three different types of industries throughout the United States (EEAC, 1982:2).

Though Equal Employment Advisory Council founders have

managed to keep the organization out of the public eye, it has sought and received recognition from the legal community. For example, it has endorsed or published several books and monographs dealing with employment discrimination and with the use of statistics in litigation and comparable worth. EEAC attorneys claim that these publications have been not only well accepted and highly regarded within the legal community, but helpful in formulating arguments presented in their briefs (McDowell, 1982). In *County of Washington v. Gunther* (1981), for example, in which the U.S. Supreme Court held that Title VII of the Civil Rights Act of 1964 was not "restricted to claims of equal pay for equal work," Justice William Brennan specifically addressed but refuted the findings reported in an EEAC publication, *Comparable Worth: Issues and Alternatives.* Thus, the EEAC has gained some recognition for its work both from legal practitioners and from individual members of the Court.

An additional sign of the Equal Employment Advisory Council's willingness to attract some attention is apparent in its interraction with like-minded groups. While EEAC attorneys do not attend the Heritage luncheons, calling them "trash," they do have some contact with several litigating groups, including the National Chamber Litigation Center and the Pacific Legal Foundation, a conservative public interest law firm. Moreover, the EEAC has recently recognized the utility of filing amicus curiae briefs with other groups, a technique it did not employ until 1981. In that year, it wrote an amicus curiae for four organizations in *Gunther.* A year later it filed another joint brief because the other organization had more expertise in the issue at hand than it did (McDowell, 1982).

One consequence of this cooperative pursuit of the amicus curiae strategy, according to one Equal Employment Advisory Council lawyer, is that their briefs are not only good but are "a lot better than they used to be" (McDowell, 1982). The EEAC believes that both the government and the justices are reading and addressing its arguments and that it is therefore having some impact on the development of employment discrimination law. While the National Chamber Litigation Center is experiencing some difficulties in deciding what strategies to use in litigation and in attracting members, the EEAC has no plans for altering its tactics. In addition, unlike the National Right to Work Legal Defense Foundation or the National Chamber Litigation Center the EEAC is not connected with a parent organization, it is relatively free to pursue litigation without the inconvenience of guarding another's interest.

Evaluating the Assumptions: Economic Interest Groups

As set forth in Chapter One, four assumptions emerge from the literature concerning interest group litigation. How well do these assumptions apply to the recent activities of conservative groups involved in economic litigation?

RESORT TO THE COURTS

The first assumption, that interest groups resort to the courts only when they are politically disadvantaged, does not accurately describe the activities of the groups investigated here. Only one of the three organizations, the National Right to Work Committee, formed a legal defense fund because it was experiencing difficulty in attaining passages of laws it wanted on the books, right-to-work laws. But even the committee had other reasons for creating its legal defense fund; the success of other groups led it to understand the utility of litigation and the frequent requests for litigation assistance it received made it well aware of the void.

This first assumption, as framed by political scientists, has even less explanatory power for the creation of the National Chamber Litigation Center and the Equal Employment Advisory Council, which formed for similar reasons — both were established because they were disadvantaged in the *judicial* arena, and not in political forums. In fact, founders of each sensed a serious void in business representation before the courts.

In sum, the first assumption has little utility in explaining the resort to the courts by economic litigators. After many decades of using the courts, many economic conservatives perceived that liberals had tipped the "scales of justice." Viewing their own interests as underrepresented in the courts, then, economic litigators were sent to fill the void. The perception of a disadvantaged status in the courts, however, appears to have prompted all three groups examined here to turn to litigation, fearing that unless their position was presented, gains won in other political spheres would be lost.

STRATEGIES

Political scientists and other scholars have concluded that direct sponsorship is the preferred strategy of interest group litigators. Although this was true of the early economic groups, the modern groups examined here have employed the range of strategic choices. National Right to Work Legal Defense Foundation attorneys, for example, have noted that sponsorship is their preferred strategy because it allows for absolute control, which they view as essential in compulsory union litigation. And although the foundation occasionally files amicus curiae briefs, like most liberal groups that use sponsorship, it does so only when its presence is viewed as critical.

The EEAC's tactics bear no likeness to the classic sponsorship approach. It participates only as an amicus curiae because its leaders view that method as cost effective, allowing it to have an impact at a much lower price. Besides, EEAC attorneys believe that amicus curiae briefs provide them with a high degree of flexibility. They are not wedded to issues they perceive as trivial and so can instead develop more fully their own perspectives in their briefs.

Because the National Chamber Litigation Center pursues a mixed strategy, using both the amicus curiae and sponsorship approaches, its participation lies between that of the National Right to Work Legal Defense Foundation and the Equal Employment Advisory Council. Because of the Chamber's negative experience during the early 1970s, the center was formed specifically to file amicus curiae briefs. But unlike the EEAC, which claims to file for impact, the center employs amicus curiae briefs in response to member requests. In fact, center staffers admit that they often file "on demand." Some of their briefs are little more than propaganda devices and are often criticized.

The National Chamber Litigation Center's current participation reveals a trend toward sponsorship of cases. The trend further substantiates O'Connor's theory that certain kinds of groups often move from the amicus curiae to the sponsorship strategy (O'Connor, 1980). The center's ability to continue to move in this direction, however, will depend on such resources as funding and staff.

For various reasons, then, each economic group has chosen to pursue a different litigation strategy. Yet there is one common thread among the three groups; whether utilizing the sponsorship, amicus, or mixed approach, each believes in the importance of creating good precedent. And, to varying degrees, all three economic litigators have demonstrated that favorable precedent can be built through any of these strategies.

RESOURCES

Scholars have assumed that interest groups can enhance their success in litigation and thus increase their impact by seeking and protecting specific resources: money, government support, group longevity, staff expertise, extra-judicial publicity, and intergroup support. A close examination of the ways economic groups have used these resources reveals the weakness of some of the traditional assumptions about interest group behavior.

Money. Financial resources are extremely important because they can determine the extent and type of involvement organizations can have in litigation. Several of the early economic groups initially experienced financial difficulties but were able to raise more money after they had achieved success in litigation. The financial status of the National Right to Work Legal Defense Foundation has followed such a pattern. Even amidst its litigation battles with the unions and the Federal Election Commission, the National Right to Work has continued to attract new members, and the additional dues have added more money to its coffers each year. Direct mail solicitation has also played an important role in its financial security. Like its parent organization, the foundation has retained the services of conservative direct mail wizard Richard Viguerie to aid in its fund-raising activities (Viguerie, 1980:38). Through direct mail campaigns conducted either with Viguerie's help or through other promotional devices, National Right to Work currently receives over $5 million per year in contributions (Viguerie, 1980:24).

The Equal Employment Advisory Council is likewise in a strong financial position. Though it has fewer members than the center, its budget is more than twice as large ($1,267,000 versus $500,000). Although the National Chamber Litigation Center is better known,

EEAC seems to be able to raise more funds because its membership includes numerous companies and associations willing to fund its activities through active fund-raising campaigns. Business Roundtable, for example, provided the $130,000 necessary to publish *Comparable Worth*, which EEAC uses as an extra-legal lobbying device.

In contrast, the National Chamber Litigation Center admits to being in financial difficulty, a predicament it blamed on the economic recession (Wieder, 1982). While even its attorneys are somewhat involved in fund raising, helping to attract new members by attending dinners and meetings with corporate general counsels, its membership has stagnated since 1981. Its inability to attract new members whose dues would increase its income may not be attributable to poor economic times, however. Unlike the Equal Employment Advisory Council or even the financially stable early conservative interest groups, the center became involved in several areas of the law. By pursuing litigation concerning union activity and employment discrimination, rather than building experience and reputation for litigation in one issue area, it may have reduced potential support. If they need to make a choice, employers may decide to contribute to the National Right to Work Legal Defense Foundation if they are concerned with union activities, or the EEAC if employment discrimination is a top priority, rather than to support the center.

The Equal Employment Advisory Council and the National Right to Work Legal Defense Foundation both appear to be financially solvent. Because of its reliance on the direct sponsorship strategy the foundation requires more funds than the EEAC, and has aggressively pursued fund-raising tactics to meet its financial needs. In contrast, the center's ability to raise money has stagnated. If the center is to continue its current trend toward using the direct sponsorship approach, it will require more financial backing to avoid the problems the Chamber encountered during its aggressive litigation period.

Government Support.   Numerous scholars have indicated how important it is for litigators to develop a rapport with the U.S. government generally, and with the Office of the Solicitor General in particular. Yet like their earlier economic counterparts, current groups have been unable to form such a relationship. Indeed, the

National Right to Work Legal Defense Foundation, like the Edison Electric Institute, has faced the wrath of the federal government in more than one instance.

The inability of these groups to muster federal support seems to be explained by two factors. First, until recently, economic litigators faced a problem similar to that of the anti-New Deal and anti-progressive groups: an inhospitable administration. President Jimmy Carter, like Franklin Roosevelt, recruited many activist attorneys to top-ranking administrative positions. David Broder tells us for example that Carter's appointee to the head of the Federal Trade Commission, Michael Pertschuk, liked to refer to the commission as the largest liberal public interest law firm in the United States (1980: 227). The Justice Department was no exception to this rule. The assistant attorney general and head of the Civil Rights Division during the Carter administration, Drew Days III, was a former NAACP Legal Defense Fund staff attorney. The presence of liberal personnel, especially in the Department of Justice, helps to explain why there was little cooperation between the economic groups and the government during the Carter administration.

Not only was there little cooperation, but the appointment of liberals to the executive branch during the Carter years also acted as a catalyst for the creation both of the Equal Employment Advisory Council and the National Chamber Litigation Center. These groups, seeing that the Carter administration would not attempt to represent business interests in court, organized to fill that void. Like several of their predecessors, including the Edison Electric Institute, they turned to litigation with the expectation that they would be challenging, instead of supporting, the government.

A second, related explanation for the absence of cooperation with the federal government concerns issue involvement. The Equal Employment Advisory Council, like the Edison Electric Institute, has attempted to monitor government policies. According to one EEAC attorney, this explicitly means that it seeks to represent business against excessively broad government regulations. While several of the groups have noted that the Reagan administration has been more sympathetic to their goals than was the Carter administration, they also believe that even a conservative presidency cannot undo the vast number of regulations that have been promulgated or the recent court decisions that have affected the business community.

The fact that cooperation between the government and the economic litigators is lacking, though contrary to the findings of scholars examining liberal groups, supports Truman's conclusions about some conservative interest groups. He discovered that conservative groups rarely participated on the same side as government because they often challenged federal legislation (1951:449). His finding, coupled with the fact that unsympathetic administrations — during the progressive, New Deal, and Carter eras — provided the catalysts for the emergence of several economic conservative interest group litigators, suggests that continued hostility between economic groups and the government is likely. In terms of government support, there appears to be a significant difference between liberal groups and conservative economic groups.

Longevity.   A third way in which interest groups presumably enhance their impact is through long-term use of the courts. By appearing continuously and more frequently before the judiciary, groups can build their reputation with the Court and thus lay a foundation upon which to build favorable precedent.

Like some of their earlier counterparts, the current economic groups have recognized the importance of increasing use of litigation, and all have attempted to increase their participation before the courts. The National Right to Work Legal Defense Foundation, for example, handled only three cases during its first year of existence. Its 1981 docket, however, included more than 250 active cases. Similarly, though participating in only four Supreme Court cases during its first year of operation, the Equal Employment Advisory Council filed more than double that number of cases decided by the Court during its 1981 term. And, since its establishment the National Chamber Litigation Center has increased its involvement to more than one hundred cases. All three groups have expanded their court agendas, revealing their awareness of the importance of building favorable precedent regardless of the strategic approach being used.

Staff.   Interest groups have often tried to increase their effectiveness in litigation by recruiting experienced and committed staff members. Like the NAACP Legal Defense Fund, for example, the

Edison Electric Institute retained the best attorneys of the day to formulate its legal arguments and to litigate its cases.

The staff of the current three economic groups are alike in several ways. First, all have a nucleus of committed staff members, many of whom have been with the organizations from the beginning. The National Right to Work Legal Defense Foundation's president, Reed Larson, was one of the members of National Right to Work Committee who pushed for the creation of the foundation. Larson, who has remained with the organization since its establishment, is currently considered one of the leaders of the New Right (Crawford, 1980:6; Viguerie, 1980:100). Richard Viguerie, says: "Reed Larson is an organizational genius who understands how to effectively use direct mail, newspaper ads, and other mass media techniques. . . . I predict Reed's efforts will persuade several new states to pass Right to Work laws in the next few years" (1980:100). The foundation's executive vice president and legal director, Rex Reed, is another long-time member of the organization. Currently, fourteen staff attorneys and more than one hundred cooperating lawyers work under Reed's direction, all of whom the foundation considers "specialists in compulsory unionism litigation" (National Right to Work, 1981:51).

The Equal Employment Advisory Council, created eight years after the National Right to Work Legal Defense Foundation, also has dedicated and well-trained staff attorneys. McGuinness worked at the NLRB, where he was familiarized with employment litigation, before he established his labor law firm. The staff attorneys at the National Chamber Litigation Center, at least through November 1982, had been with the organization since its inception. Its first executive vice president served simultaneously as the Chamber's general counsel. In 1982 litigation director Kalecyzc left the center, but was replaced by another staff attorney. While it is too early to assess the effects of this staff change, it is clear that all the economic litigators have tried to maintain stability within their respective organizations. This sort of approach, to some extent, has enabled them to cultivate expertise and to provide for some continuity in their legal programs.

Moreover, none of the three organizations has tried to inject fresh blood into their staffs through the sorts of internship or scholarship

programs run by liberal groups. And although some of the groups
claim to employ law clerks, none has established specialized programs to train law school graduates. The three groups claim that
staff stability is better than frequent change, and certainly there
are clear advantages to stability. But, as many of the liberal groups
have discovered, there are also advantages inherent in having a supply of new staffers in an organization. New attorneys often bring
with them creative and fresh ideas. Although it is too early to assess
how staff stability has affected the Equal Employment Advisory
Council and the National Chamber Litigation Center, it seems clear
that stability has allowed the National Right to Work Legal Defense Foundation to continue its litigation in a highly organized manner, which may be particularly critical for groups using a test-case
strategy.

Extra-Judicial Publicity. Another primary technique that interest groups have historically used to maximize their litigation efforts
is extra-judicial publicity, which traditionally has taken the form
of well-timed and well-placed law review articles. Two groups, the
National Right to Work Legal Defense Foundation and the Equal
Employment Advisory Council, have pursued such a course. The
foundation, for example, compiles a list of "favorable" law review
articles and collects reprints of particularly good publications. The
organization actively seeks such support because it recognizes the
important role law reviews played in the NAACP Legal Defense Fund's
victories (Reed, 1982).

In contrast, the Equal Employment Advisory Council has relied
heavily on its own publications for extra-legal publicity. Through
books either written or endorsed by EEAC attorneys, it has been able
to disseminate alternative arguments to supplement its activities in
court. Although such publications are unconventional, they have
proven very effective for the EEAC (McDowell, 1982).

The National Chamber Litigation Center has done little of this
type of lobbying. At best, it has been able to publicize its activities
in the Chamber's monthly magazine, *Nation's Business.* Because *Nation's Business* bears no resemblance to a law review it cannot be
used to disseminate legal arguments; and because it is distributed
to Chamber members, it cannot be used to gain added support for
its cause.

In sum, although the National Right to Work and the Equal Employment Advisory Council have engaged in varied kinds of publicity campaigns, the National Chamber Litigation Center has done little more than publicize its activities to an already existing cadre of supporters.

Intergroup Support. Analysts of interest group litigation have often noted the importance of another resource: support from other like-minded groups. Yet, like their predecessors, contemporary economic groups rarely support each other *in court.* Rather, all three groups — whether by choice or not — follow a carefully delineated policy of noncooperation; they purposely stay out of each other's cases in order to avoid costly and needless duplication of effort. One of the stated criteria for National Chamber Litigation Center case participation, for example, is that the business perspective is not already being adequately represented.

Adoption of this strategy makes communication among groups necessary. The Equal Employment Advisory Council and the National Chamber Litigation Center keep abreast of each other's activities by telephone, particularly in areas of overlapping interest such as affirmative action, so that they avoid filing amici in the same case. Representatives of the National Right to Work Legal Defense Foundation and the center meet monthly with other groups at the Heritage Foundation, where they too can discuss a common interest: union activity. Lack of coordination in litigation does not imply failure to cooperate outside of the courtroom. Like their predecessors who had common economically oriented interests, current economic groups have stayed out of each other's cases but have developed their own intergroup networks.

SUCCESS

The final common assumption about interest groups is that they obtain their objectives through litigation, a characterization of group behavior that flows from the numerous empirical and case studies examining the judicial activities of single groups or sets of groups. However, these studies have not considered success in the same manner because of the problems involved in measuring success. In fact, three different measures of success have emerged.

First, following in the tradition established by Clement E. Vose, some analysts have taken a group's work "as a whole" to determine if its objectives generally have been met (see, for example, Cortner, 1968; Greenberg, 1977; Manwaring, 1962; Sorauf, 1976). The logic of this approach is quite simple; according to this philosophy, a "loss" along the way may not be devastating to the attainment of overall objectives. David Manwaring, for example, demonstrated how the Jehovah's Witnesses built upon their loss in the *Minersville School District v. Gobitis* (1940) litigation to eradicate compulsory flag salutes through *West Virginia State Board of Education v. Barnette* (1943). If success was measured by actual percentages, Manwaring and others would argue, the Witnesses would have won only 50 percent of the U.S. Supreme Court flag salute cases. But of course this would be a misleading figure, because the Witnesses ultimately obtained a favorable judicial resolution of their problem.

By using this measure of success, of the three groups only the National Right to Work Legal Defense Foundation has thus far attained its goals. Through use of a test-case strategy, the foundation has severely curtailed, at least legally, the use of compulsory dues for political purposes. In contrast, neither the National Chamber Litigation Center nor the Equal Employment Advisory Council has, on the whole, met its goals. For example, both have worked to limit affirmative action programs, which were catalysts for their formations. Through the 1983 term of the Supreme Court, however, they have made little headway in this area.

Their inability to attain this and other objectives, including rejection of the comparable worth standard, may stem not only from their relative youth, but also from their reliance on the amicus curiae strategy. Unlike the Jehovah's Witnesses or even the National Right to Work Legal Defense Foundation, neither has aggressively sought to plan an overall litigation campaign; instead, their attorneys select cases from those already docketed. Although both sets of attorneys are cognizant of the importance of good precedent, they are not able to plan for future cases. The lack of a long-term perspective may help to explain why the Equal Employment Advisory Council and the National Chamber Litigation Center do not fare well on this measure.

In contrast, when a second measure of success — the percentage of cases in which the group supported the victorious party — is applied, a different picture emerges. As indicated in table 3-1, from the years the groups began litigating through the 1981 Supreme Court term, only the Equal Employment Advisory Council has supported the winning party in at least half of its cases at the Supreme Court level.

Table 3-1
Success Rates of Economic Litigators

	% of cases won*	total cases**
NRW	24%	21
NCLC	42%	26
EEAC	58%	33

Note: Data compiled by author.
*Calculated on the basis of whether the Court adopted the position advocated by the group.
**Total U.S. Supreme Court cases in which the group had been involved from the year it began litigating through the 1981 term of the Court.

While these figures are surprisingly low, they also may be misleading unless one controls for success in specific issue areas. For example, in cases involving racially based employment discrimination, in which the conservative position won 35.4 percent, the EEAC had a success rate of 50 percent, while the National Chamber Litigation Center's was 25 percent (O'Connor and Epstein, 1982b). The EEAC's win-loss rate is further enhanced when compared with that of like-minded defendants and with other groups. But without these sorts of controls, which the groups themselves do not use in calculating their own rates of success, the economic groups fared far worse than their liberal counterparts, who win more than they lose across a variety of issue areas (Baker and Asperger, 1982; Puro, 1971; O'Connor and Epstein, 1982b, 1983bc).

A final measure of success can be established by asking the groups as well as their regular opponents to assess their activities. Not surprisingly, all three economic groups claim to be successful in court, but interestingly, their assessments are based on different criteria. National Right to Work Legal Defense Foundation representatives, for example, believe they were successful because they "were absolutely changing the law" (Cameron, 1982). To illustrate: one foundation staff attorney discussed a recent compulsory dues case in which he successfully challenged a Massachusetts law. He claimed that his victory was so "devastating" that the state legislature attempted to enact legislation that would nullify the win.

In contrast, the Equal Employment Advisory Council and the National Chamber Litigation Center both point to their well-crafted briefs as measures of impact. An EEAC attorney, for example, felt certain that several U.S. Supreme Court justices and the Justice Department not only regularly read its amicus curiae briefs but actually addressed its arguments. Although the center believes its briefs had an impact, it seems more concerned with its member-businesses' belief in the importance of its participation than with the justices' favorable opinions. This sentiment is not surprising, given the center's ultimate objective, representing business interests.

Although all three groups believe they are meeting their goals through litigation, albeit for different reasons, their regular opponents disagree. The AFL-CIO, for example, has claimed that the National Right to Work Legal Defense Foundation has not accomplished a great deal and has simply relitigated well-settled issues (Pollitt, 1973). Yet the legal activities of the AFL-CIO and other unions indicate that they see the foundation as a very real threat to union ideals.

In contrast, regular opponents of the Equal Employment Advisory Council and the National Chamber Litigation Center have not been impressed by their activities. A staff attorney at the NAACP Legal Defense Fund, which regularly opposes both groups, claimed that they have "not had much force" because they make the "assumption that nothing is wrong" in the composition and regulation of the labor force. He believed that the courts generally would be unwilling to accept their arguments on the ground that the groups were neither realistic nor "historically honest" (Sherwood, 1981).

In her evaluation of the future problems facing women's groups in court, however, Margaret A. Berger suggests that women are more concerned than the NAACP Legal Defense Fund with employer organizations. Although she does not specifically mention the Equal Employment Advisory Council or the National Chamber Litigation Center, she claims: "Now that the cases are beginning to threaten the continued existence of established economic relationships which exclude women, the opposition has geared up, is digging in its heels, and is fighting every step of the way, conceding nothing" (1979:54).

Despite the variation among the economic litigators, there is a growing perception among some liberal groups that the conservatives are beginning to pose a threat in litigation. This view is obviously the case among unions, which view the National Right to Work Legal Defense Foundation — perhaps the best of the economic litigators — as a genuine threat to their survival.

Several differences between conservative economic groups and liberal groups are apparent. First, the assumption that politically disadvantaged groups resort to litigation has little utility in explaining the creation of groups to litigate economic issues. Economic litigators do not resort to the courts because they feel disadvantaged in other political forums; indeed, they actually consider themselves to be *judicially* disadvantaged. Second, even though all three groups are concerned with building precedent, they have employed the range of litigation strategies. Finally, although utilizing a wide array of resources, they have used them differently than liberal groups. Most apparent is their avoidance of cooperation in litigation and, instead, their coordination of efforts outside of the courtroom.

CONSERVATIVE SOCIAL
LITIGATION SINCE THE 1960s

At least three conservative groups were involved in social litigation during the first half of the twentieth century: the American Constitutional League, the Maryland League for State Defense, and the Sentinels of the Republic. Although these groups have ceased to exist, conservative social interests continue to be represented in court by new groups, including Citizens for Decency through Law, Americans for Effective Law Enforcement, and Americans United for Life Legal Defense Fund.

Citizens for Decency through Law

Citizens for Decency through Law, formerly Citizens for Decent Literature, was officially established in Cincinnati, Ohio in 1957. It did not use litigation until 1963, but since that year it has consistently made use of the courts.

Before 1957, the state of the law regulating obscenity was in flux. Some judges relied on the common law principle developed in *Regina v. Hicklin* (1868), which defined obscenity as anything that had the "tendency" to "deprave and corrupt" even the feeblest of minds. Others seemed to rely more heavily on Augustus Hand's more liberal standard established in *United States v. One Book Called Ulysses* (1933), which rejected the *Hicklin* test. Regardless of which test was the more relied upon, however, one fact was evident: no clear standards for defining obscenity existed, because the Supreme Court had never ruled precisely on the subject.

By the mid-1950s some saw the absence of such a ruling as a serious problem (see Gerber, 1965:120; Paul and Schwartz, 1961:83) because between 1946 and 1956 there was a "steady increase in the volume and sale of obscene material" (Barker and Barker, 1965:65). Charles H. Keating Jr., a leading Cincinnati lawyer, became very upset one day when he saw several "youngsters" at a newsstand examining what he believed was an obscene magazine. He went to the police, but though they sympathized with his anger, they claimed that there was little they could do because of the absence of legal restrictions on such of materials and because "the public" was not supportive of arrests for their display or sale.

The incident prompted Keating to study the obscenity problem. He found that many people were concerned but that their indignation typically brought only a limited response: a complaint would be filed and one store or newsstand would be "cleaned up." But Keating believed that such measures were only short-term solutions to a serious long-term problem. In 1957, convinced of the need for public pressure on law-enforcement officers, he "called together a group of business and professional friends, all fathers of young families" (Hall, 1964:95) to form a task force called Citizens for Decent Literature (CDL). Keating and members of the task force, including the chief of police of Cincinnati, began to spread their message, giving lectures on the dangers of obscenity to Parent-Teacher Associations and fraternal groups.

According to several sources (see Hall, 1964; Mark, 1965), Keating and his associates were so effective that many in their early audiences immediately called for book burnings and boycotts. But Keating and his small band of followers refused to pursue such tactics. "That's not the way . . . we have a law, and we have enforcement officials. Let's let them know we're behind them" (Hall, 1964: 95). Thus, from the start of his crusade, Keating attempted to work with law-enforcement officials to reach his objectives (see also *America*, 1959:2; Mark, 1965).

Speeches by members of Citizens for Decency through Law generated a barrage of requests to the Cincinnati police to deal with the problem, but Keating's crusade was hampered by the lack of a clear-cut, legally enforceable definition of what constituted obscenity. Although local police agreed with and in fact were part of CDL's campaign to use the law to fight obscenity, they believed that arrests at this time would be futile. This problem, however, was soon alleviated; within months of CDL's formation and initial publicity drive, the U.S. Supreme Court for the first time developed a working definition of obscenity. In *Roth v. United States* (1957), Justice William Brennan, writing for the Court, formulated the following test: "Whether to the average person applying contemporary standards the dominant theme of the material taken as a whole appeals to prurient interests" (354 U.S. at 489).

Although this new standard gave law-enforcement officials only a definition of what was obscene, Keating and Citizens for Decency through Law were relieved that the Court had dealt with the issue. After *Roth* was decided, Keating was quoted as telling Cincinnati police, "Now you can make arrests with some hope of convictions" (Hall, 1964:95). The Cincinnati Police Department seemingly concurred with Keating's remark; within the next two years, there were seven obscenity arrests and convictions in Cincinnati (*America*, 1959: 100). CDL's influence in Cincinnati became so strong that newsstand owners often requested lists of "offending magazines" from it.

Word of CDL's successes in Cincinnati soon spread throughout the country, and by 1962 the organization was barraged with requests for guidance from other communities. Because he believed the CDL had successfully dealt with the obscenity problem in Cincinnati, Keating decided in September of that year to launch a national CDL, which was initially headquartered at his law office.

This decision, almost overnight, converted Citizens for Decency through Law from a local one-office organization into a highly complex national operation. In 1963 Keating filed amicus curiae briefs in several obscenity cases then pending before the Supreme Court, one of which resulted in a full opinion. In *Jacobellis v. Ohio* (1964) CDL urged the Court to uphold a state court obscenity conviction for the showing of a "dirty movie." Writing for the Court, however, Justice Brennan, author of the *Roth* test, found that the contemporary standards requirement of the test should be conceived of as those held by "society at large."

Not only was the group filing amicus curiae briefs, but by 1964 it claimed to have greatly expanded, with three hundred "affiliated" groups. In fact, some affiliates were evidently as influential as the

Cincinnati branch (Marks, 1965:5). The Chicago Citizens for Decency through Law, for example, convinced the police department (then under the supervision of O. W. Wilson, a founder of the Americans for Effective Law Enforcement), to create "a program of attack" on obscenity. This program was "hailed as a model for police" (see Marks, 1965; Hall, 1964:98).

It was also during this early period that Keating further recognized the importance not only of working with law-enforcement officials to facilitate arrests, but of helping the prosecution to obtain convictions. The catalysts for this growing recognition of the need to supply increased help in litigation were the Supreme Court's decisions in the cases that followed *Roth*. As foreshadowed by *Jacobellis*, the Court continued to liberalize *Roth*, forcing the lower courts to acquit or to overturn convictions on the basis of its liberal language and subsequent modifications. After repeatedly watching hard-won arrests thrown out in court, Citizens for Decency through Law recognized its potentially valuable role in assisting in the conviction of those prosecuted under existing obscenity laws. To perform this function, CDL began to do a number of things almost simultaneously. First, it started to publish the biweekly *National Decency Reporter*, which contained accounts of significant obscenity cases pending throughout the United States. Such a publication was important, Keating believed, because it helped keep prosecutors informed about potentially good and innovative legal arguments.

Second, through its growing network of chapters, Citizens for Decency through Law began to develop an increasingly large pool of expert talent upon which to draw. CDL used this network to make "available to local prosecutors expert psychiatric and social testimony on the affects of obscene publications" (Hall, 1964:96; Marks, 1965:6). For example, pediatrician William P. Reilly, president of the New York CDL and vice president of the national CDL, provided testimony for the prosecution in *Memoirs v. Massachusetts* (1966). He testified as to why *Fanny Hill*, (John Cleland's *Memoirs of a Woman of Pleasure*) would have a detrimental effect on the "average person" (Rembar, 1968:344–54). And in addition to providing expert testimony for prosecutors, the CDL network continued to pressure both police and prosecutors to deal more effectively with local obscenity problems.

Finally, Citizens for Decency through Law continued its involvement in litigation by filing amicus briefs at the Supreme Court level. Not only would amicus curiae briefs be the least expensive way to affect the Court, Keating felt, but this type of participation helped meet CDL's general goal of working with law-enforcement officials. To facilitate this sort of participation, in 1965 Keating hired James C. Clancy, a former deputy district attorney in Los Angeles to serve as legal counsel and as the only salaried member of CDL (Junk, 1965: 360).

The addition of Clancy to Citizens for Decency through Law was well timed, for by 1965 several major obscenity cases were pending for hearing by the U.S. Supreme Court. One of the most important of these was *Memoirs*, in which the Court was asked to decide whether *Fanny Hill* could be considered obscene under the *Roth* test, because only certain portions of the book were alleged to be obscene. CDL had already contributed to the litigation through Reilly's testimony. But because it recognized the potential importance of the case, CDL wanted to increase its participation even further, and so when the case reached the high court Clancy and Keating prepared an amicus curiae brief. The plaintiff's attorney, Charles Rembar, denied CDL's request to file the brief, but the Court granted its petition.[1] In retrospect, Rembar was grateful that the Court allowed CDL to file an amicus curiae. He later claimed: "The Citizens' arguments were quite different from those of the attorney general, and we had to write a separate set of briefs to meet them. But where our friends, I thought, might have done us harm, our enemies were helpful" (Rembar, 1968:423). A close examination of CDL's brief in *Memoirs* supports Rembar's comments. Keating and Clancy presented highly emotional, not legal, arguments to the Court. They cited only one obscenity case, one decided during King George II's reign in England. The CDL brief's rather unprofessional tenor enabled Rembar to use it to his advantage. During oral argument, for example, he implied that if the justices ruled against his client, they would be deciding in favor of CDL (see Rembar, 1968: 459–60). Given the arguments and the Court's inclination to expand the definition of obscenity, it was not surprising that in *Fanny Hill*, the Court further liberalized the *Roth* test by adding the phrase "utterly without redeeming social value."

CDL's litigation efforts in *Fanny Hill* and in several other cases decided between the mid-1960s and the early 1970s were unsuccessful.[2] Moreover, its other activities also came under attack. Some began to suggest that CDL representatives placed undue pressure on prosecutors. According to one observer, "Lawyers have complained that after several CDL members spend hours in a public official's office arguing against smut, it seems that a large segment of the community is up in arms. The official gets an inflated opinion of the support for anti-smut campaigns" (Mark, 1965:6). Some attorneys also expressed disdain for CDL publicity, which usually took the form of pamphlets for circulating propaganda on pending cases. For example, after a lower court's decision involving an allegedly obscene book, *Tropic of Cancer*, CDL issued a pamphlet consisting of its "dirtiest" passages. According to Elmer Gertz, a defense attorney, "this pamphlet, which was supposed to show how bad the book was, had no plot, no redeeming qualities. While fighting pornography, CDL had actually created a piece of pornography" (quoted in Mark, 1965:6). In *Hayse v. Van Hoomissen* (1970), in fact, the district court judge, who was striking an Oregon obscenity law, asserted, "Under the broad language just quoted, the citizen who fills his briefcase with obscene samples and carries them to a Citizens for Decent Literature meeting to reinforce that organization's anxieties will risk criminal prosecution along with those who pander the material commercially in public" (321 F. Supp. at 645).

Such attacks, which continued unabated through the mid-1970s, generally emanated from Citizens for Decency through Law opponents and little affected its dedicated supporters. The constant criticism may actually have helped draw attention to the organization and its founder. Because Keating had developed a reputation as "the" smut fighter through his work at CDL, President Richard Nixon appointed him to the Federal Commission on Obscenity and Pornography when a vacancy arose in 1969. The commission, which was established by Congress in July 1968 to "investigate the effect of pornography on social behavior, to determine the need for new laws and to report on the constitutionality of such laws" (Halloran, 1970a: 42), had been composed exclusively of Lyndon Johnson appointees, most of whom were sympathetic to the civil libertarian side of the debate.

It was not long before Keating's "minority" position on the commission attracted media attention. The press constantly referred to him as "the most controversial member of the commission" (see, for example, Halloran, 1970a:42), a title that was underscored when Keating attempted to prevent publication of the majority report. Because he disagreed with the report's findings, particularly the recommendation that all obscenity laws "pertaining to 'consenting adults' be repealed," Keating brought suit in federal court in 1970 to stop its publication (Halloran, 1970b:8). After a temporary restraining order was issued, Keating met with a Justice Department attorney who represented the commission, and they negotiated a compromise: the report would be published, but Keating would be permitted to file a dissent (*New York Times*, 15 September 1970:23; see *Obscenity Report*, 1971:194–216, for Keating's position). Interestingly, instead of adopting the commission's majority report, both President Nixon and the Senate endorsed the Keating dissent.

Keating's involvement in the commission not only drew attention to Citizens for Decency through Law, but also reaffirmed his belief that the battle against obscenity was far from over. But to conduct a more intense campaign, Keating knew he had to obtain greater financial support. In 1971 CDL, like many other conservative groups hired Richard Viguerie to raise funds. Given the free publicity CDL had already enjoyed because of its tactics and Keating's stint on the commission, Viguerie's task was not difficult. Over the next two years his organization raised more than $2.3 million in the name of CDL.[3]

With this sort of financial backing and publicity, Citizens for Decency through Law began to make several internal changes, all geared to making its litigation more effective. First, it began to cultivate a more professional legal staff, which Keating brought to CDL's newly established headquarters in Phoenix, Arizona. In light of CDL's poor showing in the Court, Keating recognized that it needed not only to increase the size of its legal staff but also to bring in attorneys skilled in obscenity litigation from the government perspective. By 1980 CDL had hired several staff attorneys, including two former government prosecutors: Bruce A. Taylor, a former member of the Cleveland prosecutor's office and CDL's current general counsel, and Faye M. Gardner, a U.S. attorney from Pittsburgh. (Clancy continues to provide legal services to CDL, but he is currently working in Los Angeles [McCommon, 1983].)

Second, CDL established a National Center for Decency at its

Phoenix headquarters. The center is designed to assist attorneys, making available to them "both historic and current data regarding pornography's impact on society" (CDL, n.d.), information that attorneys can use in formulating their arguments. The center has lent credence to CDL's claim that it is "the clearinghouse" for legal information on the obscenity "problem" (McCommon, 1983).

Finally, armed with financial backing and a higher level of legal expertise, CDL has widened its strategic focus to include participation both as an amicus curiae and as direct sponsor. How much it has expanded its litigation activities is revealed in its most recent court docket. In *New York v. Ferber* (1982) CDL attorneys, including Taylor, Gardner, and Keating, filed an amicus curiae brief urging the Supreme Court to declare that "'child pornography' [is] inherently unprotected by the First Amendment, because it is obscene as a matter of law" (CDL, October 1982:6). Their arguments, unlike those CDL presented in earlier briefs, were based on Supreme Court precedents and were written in a concise legalistic manner, without emotional appeal. And in contrast to its early cases, in which the Court explicitly rejected CDL arguments, in *Ferber* it held that the New York law outlawing child pornography "sufficiently describes a category of material the production and distribution of which is not entitled to First Amendment protection" (73 L. Ed. 2d 1128). Thus, CDL not only won the case, but its arguments were incorporated into the Court's opinion.

While Citizens for Decency through Law has continued to file amicus curiae briefs, the "connections" of its newly formulated legal staff have allowed it to pursue the sponsorship strategy with increasing regularity. Just one year before *Ferber*, in *Flynt v. Ohio* (1981), the state hired Taylor to represent it in its case against Larry Flynt's *Hustler* magazine. Taylor was believed to be the best attorney to represent the state because he was the city prosecutor at the time of Flynt's arrest. While the trial court dismissed Ohio's complaint on the ground that Flynt had been "subjected to selective and discriminatory prosecution," Taylor won in the U.S. Supreme Court. There the Court affirmed the Supreme Court of Ohio, which had remanded the case for trial.

Although CDL attorneys have stated that they do not necessarily prefer this tactic to the amicus curiae (McCommon, 1983), they often feel that their assistance is critical because "with their heavy and diverse case load, most local prosecutors cannot become experts in obscenity law. Often they are defeated in court, not because the law is not on their side, but because they lack the resources and expertise to effectively enforce the law" (CDL, n.d.). Like the National Consumers' League, which cosponsored cases with states when protective legislation was challenged, CDL attempts to represent states or local governments at the trial court level because it believes that its attorneys can provide their full attention to the litigation. However, its attorneys claim that they "don't try to force their way" into cases (McCommon, 1983).

In some cases that Citizens for Decency through Law has not been specifically asked to handle as a direct sponsor, it has offered or has been asked to provide assistance as an intervenor—"a person [or group] who voluntarily interposes in an action . . . with leave of the Court" (Black, 1968:956). The intervention strategy itself has been controversial. Several scholars claim that procedural problems, particularly the "timeliness" of applications for intervention, often hamper the ability of groups to participate as intervenors (see Shapiro, 1968: Stern and Gressman, 1978). Others, however, suggest that interest groups would be wise to rely more heavily on intervention, especially if they find that their views are inadequately represented by the sponsoring parties (see Jones, 1979, 1980; Weinstein, 1980). The latter view well describes CDL's attitude toward the intervention approach. For example, in *U.S. Marketing v. Idaho* (1982), a case involving a bookstore allegedly dealing in obscene materials, CDL attorneys intervened at the request of the state (McCommon, 1983). According to CDL, in cases such as *U.S. Marketing*, prosecutors are more "than happy to get assistance" given their often heavy work loads.

Citizens for Decency through Law began using litigation in the early 1960s, but its briefs generally had little effect and, in fact, may have helped the opposition because they were overtly emotional and nonlegalistic. During the early 1970s, however, the organization set out to increase and professionalize its litigation efforts. It hired several attorneys who had experience as local prosecutors in obscenity litigation and who steered the organization in new directions. Given the maintenance of a good legal staff, CDL plans to continue and perhaps further improve its use of the courts.

Americans for Effective Law Enforcement

Like Citizens for Decency through Law, Americans for Effective Law Enforcement (AELE) is a socially conservative group that uses litigation as a primary lobbying device. In contrast to CDL, however, AELE was established in response to a specific set of U.S. Supreme Court decisions and to the circumstances surrounding those decisions, and not in response to the absence of legal doctrine.

Beginning in the early 1960s, the United States Supreme Court under the leadership of Chief Justice Earl Warren "revolutionized" criminal law and procedure. Many scholars have pinpointed the Court's decision in *Mapp. v. Ohio* (1961) as the beginning of the criminal rights "revolution." In that case the Court held that the exclusionary rule, as developed in *Weeks v. United States* (1914), was applicable to the states through the Fourteenth Amendment. The liberal trend in criminal rights continued almost unabated during the decade of the 1960s. In *Gideon v. Wainwright* (1963) the Court incorporated the Sixth Amendment guarantee of the right to counsel. Three years later, in *Miranda v. Arizona* (1966), the Court held that suspects must be given four warnings, which have come to be called "*Miranda* warnings," at the time of arrest.

While liberal groups, including the American Civil Liberties Union (ACLU), which had filed an amicus curiae brief in *Miranda* and in many of the other criminal cases, applauded the Warren Court's decisions as important constitutional safeguards for the accused, these decisions were very unpopular among conservatives and law-enforcement officials. For Fred Inbau, a renowned criminal procedure scholar from the Northwestern University Law School, *Miranda* and the other Warren Court decisions acted as catalysts for his decision to establish Americans for Effective Law Enforcement in Chicago in 1966. He and several other colleagues, including James R. Thompson, the current governor of Illinois, in conjunction with law-enforcement officials including O. W. Wilson, who had assisted the Chicago Citizens for Decency through Law, recognized the need to respond "to the success that the ACLU and other civil liberties groups were having" (Graham, 1972:26). They organized AELE specifically to litigate on behalf of "law-abiding citizens" of the United States (AELE, n.d., a).

While Americans for Effective Law Enforcement was officially incorporated in 1967, during its early years it was "very much a hip-pocket operation" under the direction of Inbau (*Newsweek*, 1972: 31). Its inability to function fully seemingly stemmed from a high concern during this period for the rights of the accused, which translated into a lack of financial support for those concerned with law enforcement. During this early period, however, AELE managed to obtain sufficient support to file an amicus curiae in one U.S. Supreme Court case: *Terry v. Ohio* (1968).

Americans for Effective Law Enforcement's amicus curiae in *Terry* was a surprisingly professional effort, given that it was its first appearance in the Court. Preparing the brief for AELE, Thompson paid careful attention to the issue at hand — whether police, for their own well-being, could stop and frisk individuals suspected of potentially committing crimes. Reflecting his academic background, Thompson's brief cited relevant precedents and law review articles and was to the point, without emotionalism. And unlike the CDL, whose early briefs failed to address arguments presented by other amici or parties, AELE's brief specifically addressed arguments put forth by the NAACP, an amicus curiae on Terry's side. Not only did *Terry* represent the type of case in which AELE most wanted to become involved, but in its first appearance it attempted to live up to its purpose by counterbalancing the arguments of a liberal opponent. And in 1968 the Warren Court agreed with AELE, upholding the limited stop-and-frisk interrogation at issue in *Terry*, which constituted a rare departure from its liberal stance in this area of the law.

With this win in hand, Inbau and Americans for Effective Law Enforcement began to command some national recognition, which coincided with the election of Nixon in 1968. Nixon, who had run on a "law and order stance," almost immediately began to show his support for AELE goals. Inbau, for example, was often "invited to the White House for the signing of anti-crime legislation" (Graham, 1972:26). In addition, AELE received a substantial contribution from W. Clement Stone, a major financial supporter of Nixon and the Republican party. In January of 1971, the administration's position toward AELE was even further solidified when Attorney General John Mitchell formally endorsed AELE's activities (Smith, 1971) in a letter "declar[ing] his support for the . . . group to 'represent the legitimate interests of law enforcement and our law-abiding citizens'" (Graham, 1972).

This endorsement was merely icing on the cake for Americans for Effective Law Enforcement members. By the time Mitchell voiced the official approval of the administration, AELE had already raised levels in its coffers substantially through Inbau's less formal connections with the administration and other sources. Five months before Mitchell's endorsement, in fact, AELE had raised enough money to hire a full-time executive director, Frank Carrington. Carrington was an attorney who had served as a law-enforcement officer for ten years after graduating from the University of Michigan Law School and taking a Master of Laws degree in criminal law at Northwestern University (Carrington, 1975).

Once Carrington was hired, Americans for Effective Law Enforcement immediately increased its litigation activities at the Supreme Court level. Like the Equal Employment Advisory Council, AELE has participated solely as an amicus curiae in litigation. Its reasons for utilizing this tactic are twofold. First, like the EEAC, AELE believes that amicus curiae briefs, as the one filed in *Terry* best exemplifies, can not only have an impact on the Court but help establish precedent or whittle away at adverse rulings in already docketed cases. Inbau, for example, has noted:

> We can't choose what cases to take to the high court: the justices do. We can only hope appropriate cases get up there. We can only select cases from those that the Court has agreed to consider. We can't continually repeat a "We told you so" response and file a rubber stamp brief. We seek to retain the Court's interest and hope to systematically lead a majority of Justices to the point where the cumulative body of case law favors our position. [AELE, n.d., b]

A second explanation for Americans for Effective Law Enforcement's reliance on the amicus curiae strategy is that it cannot directly sponsor cases without permission from state or federal prosecutors. In contrast to Citizens for Decency through Law, which faces a similar problem, AELE has not sought to pursue this or the intervention approach because it believes that "it is the duty of a prosecutor to request a reviewing court to uphold a conviction or to find that a state statute is constitutional. An amicus organization is looking at the 'big picture' concerning legal principles" (AELE, n.d., b). Unlike CDL, AELE believes that the prosecution generally performs its function admirably. AELE attorneys realize, however, that the prosecution is generally most concerned with securing "a" conviction, and it is therefore up to them to help build favorable precedent by providing a long-term view of the litigation.

Americans for Effective Law Enforcement's docket is replete with examples in all areas of criminal law of ways this strategy has worked successfully. For example, AELE leaders strongly voiced their support of the Supreme Court's decision in *Chambers v. Maroney* (1970), in which the Court upheld the search without a warrant of a car impounded incident to an arrest. Because AELE was cognizant of the controversy surrounding the Court's decision, it attempted to file amicus curiae briefs in several of the later car search cases, including *South Dakota v. Opperman* (1976) and *United States v. Ross* (1982), to help reinforce the validity of such searches.

South Dakota v. Opperman was one of the first post-*Maroney* cases decided by the Court. In *Opperman* the Court was asked to determine whether an automobile that had been illegally parked and subsequently impounded could be searched without a warrant. In its brief Americans for Effective Law Enforcement presented two arguments supporting the state. First, it claimed that "the inventory of the contents of a lawfully impounded automobile is a proper procedure for the safeguarding of the property of the owner and the protection of the police" (AELE, 1975:5). To support this point AELE conducted a survey of two hundred "law enforcement agencies" that indicated that vehicle inventories rarely helped police to obtain evidence. Second, based on *Maroney* and other U.S. Supreme Court precedents, AELE argued that the evidence found in the *Opperman* inventory should be admissible because cars presented a special exception to search-and-seizure limitations.

The Court adopted these arguments in full. Writing for the Court, Chief Justice Burger seemed to rely on AELE's survey, concluding that "in following standard police procedures prevailing throughout the country and approved by the majority of the courts, the conduct of the police was not 'unreasonable' under the Fourth Amendment" (428 U.S. at 376).

While *Opperman* was a major victory for Americans for Effective Law Enforcement because it indicated the Court's willingness to abide by the *Maroney* precedent, car search cases became much more complex during the next few years. Between 1976 and 1981, the U.S. Supreme Court was asked to determine how far police could go in searching an automobile without a warrant. In many of these cases AELE attempted to convince the Court to adopt a rule that would allow the police to search containers found in a car so long as "the prerequisites for a search have been established" (AELE, 1980:3).

But until 1982 the Supreme Court was reluctant to go that far. Although it ruled that certain types of containers could be freely searched, it prohibited warrantless searches of locked glove compartments. In *United States v. Ross*, however, the Court abandoned those distinctions and adopted arguments that Americans for Effective Law Enforcement had presented not only in the instant case, but that it had used all along in an attempt to build favorable precedent in this area of the law. In *Ross*, AELE asked the Court to make a "clear cut pronouncement . . . that once there is probable cause to search a car, the police may search any container within any part of the car" (AELE, 1980:3). Writing for the Court, Justice Stevens noted:

> We hold that the scope of the warrantless search authorized by that exception is no broader and no narrower than a magistrate could legitimately authorize by warrant. If probable cause justifies the search of a lawfully stopped vehicle, it justifies the search of *every part of the vehicle* and its contents that may conceal the object of the search. [72 L. Ed. 2d at 594, emphasis added]

Once Americans for Effective Law Enforcement had helped to establish the *Opperman* precedent, it built upon that by continuing to ask the Court to move beyond *Opperman's* scope. Its perseverance, of course, coupled with the Court's continued conservatism in the area of criminal rights, led to a major victory in *Ross*.

Beyond AELE's ability to use the amicus curiae as others have employed the direct sponsorship approach — to build favorable precedent — its amicus curiae participation is noteworthy for several reasons. First, unlike the Equal Employment Advisory Council, AELE generally submits joint amicus curiae briefs on behalf of national organizations, including the International Association of Police Chiefs and the National District Attorneys Association, and state and local groups, such as the California Law Enforcement Legal Advisors Association and the Wyoming Sheriffs' Association. In addition, it is one of only a handful of organizations whose amicus curiae briefs are regularly joined by state attorneys general. AELE claims that this sort of cooperative participation is possible because the groups or the states have a common purpose: "a concern for the fair and effective enforcement of criminal law."

Second, Americans for Effective Law Enforcement has not veered from its original goal of acting as a counterbalance to civil libertarian groups through amicus curiae participation. It makes every effort to participate in cases in which the ACLU is supporting the alleged perpetrator. In reporting its participation in *Allen v. Mc-Curry* (1980), a case involving the question of whether a convicted inmate could relitigate a claim of an illegal search and seizure, AELE claimed that the "city attorney appealed to the United States Supreme Court and asked AELE to file a friend of the court brief. The American Civil Liberties Union filed a brief on the other side" (AELE, n.d., b:3).

A final trend evident in Americans for Effective Law Enforcement's briefs is its utilization of statistics and of law review articles written by Inbau and other AELE members. Like the NAACP Legal Defense Fund, AELE's use of these techniques has helped to reinforce its legal arguments, as evident in *Opperman.*

Unlike Citizens for Decency through Law, which took several years to establish itself as a serious litigator, Americans for Effective Law Enforcement almost from the beginning had no difficulty in establishing a professional reputation. Under the initial directorship of Inbau, who was already well respected in legal circles, the organization not only has established ties with various groups, states, and the federal government but has also helped to build favorable precedents in the area of criminal rights.

Americans United for Life Legal Defense Fund

Unlike Citizens for Decency through Law or Americans for Effective Law Enforcement, Americans United for Life Legal Defense Fund is the litigating arm for its parent organization, Americans United for Life (AUL). It is also reputed to be "the" legal arm of the entire anti-abortion movement.[4] Thus, its establishment and subsequent activities are best understood in the context of those of AUL in particular, and of the entire anti-abortion movement more generally.

Americans United for Life was founded in 1971 in the midst of the abortion debate in the United States, as groups on both sides of the issue were waging major battles in legislative corridors, lobbying to promote their respective interests. During this time many of the organizations that advocated a pro-choice stance, such as the American Civil Liberties Union, Planned Parenthood, and the National Abortion Rights Action League, had abandoned their earlier posture calling for reform of old abortion laws. Instead, they began to call for repeal of all restrictive state laws (see generally, Lader, 1973; Hole and Levine, 1971; Rubin, 1982).

As these and like-minded groups began to make some headway in the state legislatures, a strong anti-abortion movement was mounted. At first, this countermovement was conducted almost exclusively by the Roman Catholic Church. But by 1971 the Church began to receive some organizational support; small grass-roots groups sprang up across the United States to lobby against repeal. One such group was Americans United for Life, which began as an educational organization in Washington, D.C. (Marzen, 1983). Shortly thereafter it moved to Chicago, where it could be closer to the several physicians, members of the clergy, and professors of religion and of law who were instrumental in its creation. (Among those were Northwestern University Law School professor Victor G. Rosenblum and its future chair, Dennis J. Horan [Marzen, 1983].) Like the other small anti-abortion groups forming at this time, AUL lobbied against repeal and also continued to educate the public on "the harmful effects of induced abortion" (Balides et al., 1973:511) through the dissemination of books and articles.

The impact of Americans United for Life, other grass-roots organizations, and the Catholic Church on the repeal campaign of pro-choice groups was tremendous. Between 1969 and 1972, only four states—New York, Hawaii, Alaska, and Colorado—repealed or liberalized their restrictive laws. And even in those states where pro-choice forces won, they faced uphill struggles. In retrospect, however, anti-abortion groups may have been too successful; they forced pro-choice groups to resort to litigation, which turned out to be a powerful political weapon. One commentator, in fact, claimed that "during 1970 and 1971, an avalanche of cases came before all levels of courts" (Potts et al., 1977:343; see also Rubin, 1982:41–43), challenging restrictive abortion practices that legislatures refused to alter.

Two cases that were part of this "avalanche" were *Roe v. Wade* and *Doe v. Bolton* (both 1973). Although *Roe* and *Doe* challenged different types of abortion laws, their court histories were remarkably similar. *Roe* challenged an 1857 Texas law that permitted abortions only "by medical advice for the purpose of saving the life of the mother." *Doe*, initiated by the Georgia ACLU, presented a challenge to that state's law, which required that an abortion be performed in a state-accredited hospital, that the operation be approved by a medical committee, and that two other doctors had to concur with the "attending physician's judgment." Both suits were heard by three-judge district courts in 1970, but neither court issued an injunction against enforcement of the laws. Attorneys for both *Roe* and *Doe* appealed to the U.S. Supreme Court, which agreed to hear arguments.

Once the Supreme Court accepted the cases for review, both sides had an opportunity to gather support. The pro-choice side attracted significant amicus curiae support. The more than twenty briefs not only helped to show how widespread the support was, but several amici curiae apparently influenced the Court's decision. In his majority opinion, for example, Justice Harry Blackmun referred to several pro-choice amici curiae, including one submitted by the American Public Health Association.

Although anti-abortion groups also had the opportunity to gain support for their cause, their success was limited. The Texas and Georgia cases were supported by amicus curiae briefs from seven states, all of which had restrictive abortion laws; by two anti-abortion groups, Americans United for Life and the League for Infants, Fetuses and the Elderly (LIFE); and by a coalition of interests led by Women for the Unborn.

Not only was this a relatively small show of support for the anti-abortion position, but the amici made morally based arguments that were unable to counter the medical, statistical, and legal information presented by pro-choice groups. In its ten-page brief, for example, Americans United for Life claimed:

> We are not concerned . . . with the question of whether a state law can constitutionally allow abortion where it is necessary to save the life of the mother. Rather the issue is whether the constitution permits the child in the womb to be killed where it is not necessary to save the life of

his mother. To permit the child in the womb to be killed in such a case improperly discriminates against him on account of his age and situation.

Writing for the seven-member majority, Justice Blackmun rejected AUL's and other anti-abortion arguments, concluding that the right of a woman to obtain an abortion is included in her right to privacy. The Court found that during the first trimester of pregnancy, a woman's right to privacy outweighs a state's interest in protecting her health. From the end of the first trimester to "viability," a state cannot prohibit an abortion, but it can "reasonably regulate." After viability, a state can prohibit an abortion except when it is necessary to protect a woman's health. The decision of the Court in *Roe* struck down the abortion laws of thirty-one states.

In *Doe* the Court reviewed the constitutionality of state abortion restrictions. It found that requiring a medical committee's approval, doctors' concurrences, and residency and hospital-accreditation regulations was unconstitutional. The Court also held that abortion decisions made during the first trimester were private, between a woman and her doctor. *Doe* effectively invalidated the abortion laws of fifteen states.

The various groups that had fought for legalized abortion services achieved their goal in 1973. Given that litigation efforts did not commence until the late 1960s, their objective had been met rapidly. Many pro-choice attorneys and groups believed the battle had finally ended.

For anti-abortion forces, including Americans United for Life, however, the abortion controversy took on new meaning. Prior to *Roe* and *Doe*, anti-abortion groups had successfully lobbied against repeal. Now that those legislative victories had no meaning, groups opposed to abortion had no choice but to fight the Court's decision. *Roe* and *Doe* acted as catalysts for the formation of the right-to-life movement (see Merton, 1981; Rubin, 1982).

After 1973, legislative lobbying was the first tack followed by most anti-abortion forces. Ultimately, they set their sights on a human life amendment that would effectively overturn the Court's decisions (English, 1981:18). Realistically, however, they hoped to limit abortion services in any way they could. Thus, they lobbied state legislatures and localities to secure the passage of limitations on two issues not addressed by *Roe* and *Doe:* consent requirements and funding for abortion services. By targeting these areas, as well as by lobbying for a constitutional amendment, these groups have attempted to limit the scope of *Roe* and *Doe.*

While the vast majority of the anti-abortion groups, including Americans United for Life, began to lobby legislatures, AUL began to consider the possibility of using litigation. As one of the few anti-abortion groups involved in *Roe*, it saw the success of liberal groups and wondered if it could use the courts to similar advantage. Furthermore, it recognized that like-minded groups would need litigation support when their attempts at restricting the scope of *Roe* were challenged by pro-choice forces.

In 1975, Americans United for Life members began to assemble a "loose knit" group of anti-abortion attorneys who were to examine the possibility of regular, sustained litigation (Marzen, 1983). Included in this group were Patrick A. Trueman, a law student and future director of AUL Legal Defense Fund; John Gorby, a professor at John Marshall Law School in Chicago; and David W. Louisdell, the Elizabeth Jocelyn Boalt Professor of Law at the University of California at Berkeley. This group also received support from Horan and Rosenblum.

Because their lack of experience and confidence in using litigation in the abortion area, the group decided against going directly to court, which was not surprising after *Roe*. Instead, it chose to contact a state attorney about his involvement in a pending case in which a Chicago man was accused of shooting a pregnant woman, killing the fetus and wounding her. Upon discovering that the man had not been charged for the murder of the woman's "unborn child," the Americans United for Life group "lobbied" the state attorney, who eventually upped the charge to include murder.

While the defendant was acquitted on all counts, Americans United for Life was "encouraged" by its ability to place pressure on the state attorney. "This convinced me that our group could have an impact on the legal system," Trueman declared (quoted in Strobel, 1980). Armed with renewed confidence in using litigation, however indirectly, the AUL in 1975 made plans to formalize the organization by incorporating as a tax-exempt legal defense fund. Louisdell was name project director and the original loosely knit group pledged its support.

With this base of attorneys, the newly established Americans United for Life Legal Defense Fund sought almost immediately to build a cooperating network of sympathetic attorneys around the United States. This was a top priority, because the fund recognized the need for the defense of restrictive abortion legislation throughout the country, in view of the grass-roots strategy of the anti-abortion movement. The building of this network was facilitated by the professional connections of its original advocates, and also by the group's decision to begin publication immediately of a newsletter, *Lex Vitae*, that contained a summary of pending abortion cases and was mailed to attorneys across the United States. Since 1975, this publication has become "the" abortion docket of anti-abortion forces. Like that published by the pro-choice Reproductive Freedom Project of the ACLU (see Epstein, 1982; Gelb and Palley, 1982), AUL Legal Defense Fund's docket has served the important function of keeping potentially sympathetic attorneys abreast of all pending cases.

While the AUL Legal Defense Fund was attempting to establish itself by building an attorney network and publishing an abortion docket, it was faced with a lack of financial resources needed to pursue litigation. To attract monetary support, representatives of the organization asked other anti-abortion groups to provide funding, promising in return to act as "the" legal representative of the movement. These groups, in turn, began to contribute when they realized that their legislative lobbying victories needed court support. From the beginning the AUL Legal Defense Fund developed a symbiotic relationship with the other anti-abortion groups; it promised to support their legislative victories, particularly in the areas of funding and consent restrictions, in return for financial support. Currently, the fund claims to receive contributions from more than two hundred anti-abortion groups and maintain contact with seven hundred national and local organizations.

To a large extent, the fund has lived up to its promise. An AUL fund attorney has claimed that since its establishment "there's hardly an abortion case around the country of any significance in which we don't have some impact either by giving advice or written material"(Strobel, 1980). But while the fund has become "the" representative of anti-abortion forces in court, its early litigation efforts were unsuccessful. In general, its initial briefs were hampered by the same

problem they had in *Roe;* their arguments were too emotional, relying heavily on morality instead of legality (Marzen, 1983). In litigation that immediately followed *Roe,* moreover, the AUL Legal
Defense Fund attempted to convince the Supreme Court to overrule its 1973 decisions, rather than to whittle away those precedents
gradually.

These problems were clearly evident in one of the fund's first cases,
Planned Parenthood v. Danforth (1976). At issue in *Danforth* was
a Missouri consent statute, which, among other provisions, required
the written consent of a pregnant woman, or her spouse, or (in the
case of an unmarried minor) her parents, prior to the performance
of an abortion. The law was designed and heavily lobbied for by
a coalition of anti-abortion forces as a way to limit the impact of
Roe and *Doe,* but it was quickly challenged by Planned Parenthood's
Missouri affiliate, which was represented by the ACLU.

It was the responsibility of the attorney general of Missouri, John
Danforth, to argue the case, but the AUL Legal Defense Fund filed
an amicus curiae brief to begin to establish its reputation as "the"
legal arm of the anti-abortion movement. Written by Horan and
Gorby, the brief was filed on behalf of Americans United for Life
and Dr. Eugene Diamond, an AUL board member, who had been
"appointed guardian ad litem for the class of unborn children" in
a similar case pending in an Illinois district court (AUL, 1975:4).

While Attorney General Danforth presented crisp legal arguments, focusing on why the Missouri law was consistent with *Roe*
and *Doe,* AUL Legal Defense Fund attorneys were overtly emotional
in tone. Like the early briefs of Citizens for Decency through Law,
the fund's brief seemingly helped the ACLU's case. Because it argued
for a limitation or an overruling of *Roe* (going so far as to compare
Roe with *Dred Scott v. Sandford* [1857]), instead of reinforcing Danforth's position, the fund merely lent credence to the ACLU's argument that the Missouri law would curtail the scope of *Roe.* Thus,
instead of supplementing government arguments, providing a solid
counterbalance to the liberal position, or even presenting the Court
with new or useful information, as indicated by the *Danforth* brief,
the AUL Legal Defense Fund's early briefs tended to underscore the
emotional aspects of the issue.

A year after *Danforth* was decided, however, Americans United
for Life and its Legal Defense Fund underwent several staff changes.

Its chair, Professor George H. Williams, resigned "because of the pressure of academic duties" at Harvard (AUL, 8 December 1977:6). He was replaced by Dennis Horan, who always had a special interest in the legal defense program. During the same year, the fund's project director, Louisdell, died. He was replaced by Patrick Trueman, a member of the original AUL legal group.

These personnel changes, like those made by Citizens for Decency through Law in the late 1970s, seemed to help the AUL Legal Defense Fund. The new leaders apparently understood the group's earlier litigation mistakes and stood to profit from them. Trueman has conceded that a "certain amount" of "emotionalism . . . crept into the group's early work" (Strobel, 1980:6). Other staff members have agreed with this assessment, noting that early AUL Legal Defense Fund efforts were sloppy and intensely ideological (Marzen, 1983). Recognition of the lack of professionalism led the fund to make a number of strategic changes that were similar to those made by CDL in the late 1970s and early 1980s. Although the AUL Legal Defense Fund has continued to represent and act as the "legal backup" of anti-abortion forces, its briefs have taken on a more professional and legal tenor.

Its amicus curiae brief in *H.L. v. Matheson* (1981), which supported a Utah law "requiring a doctor to notify, if possible" a minor's parents prior to an abortion, illustrates the Legal Defense Fund's changing "look." Rather than emphasizing the emotional/moral aspects of the issue or asking the Court to overrule *Roe*, AUL Legal Defense Fund attorneys noted:

> The Utah law now before this Court differs substantially from the . . .
> Missouri parent consent laws in *Planned Parenthood v. Danforth* . . . .
> it merely provides notice to parents that their minor daughter is seeking an abortion.
> This notification does not violate any primary right against public disclosure, since the minor's parents are not members of the general public, but rather guardians with responsibility for her care and nurture. [AUL, 1980:3]

In its brief AUL Legal Defense Fund presented well-crafted legal arguments, focusing on how the Utah law differed from those the Court previously rejected. Writing for the Court, Chief Justice Burger reflected the AUL Legal Defense Fund's argument: "As applied to the class properly before us, the statute plainly serves important states' interests, is narrowly drawn to protect only those interests, and does not violate any guarantees of the Constitution" (450 U.S. at 413). Besides toning down their emotionalism and presenting the Court with more legally based arguments, the fund's briefs have also become more "patient"—rather than asking the Court to overrule *Roe*, they attempted to whittle away the precedent.

A second change in fund strategy occurring after 1977 concerned its mode of participation. Since its establishment the fund had relied almost exclusively on the amicus curiae strategy. Like Citizens for Decency through Law attorneys, however, those at the AUL Legal Defense Fund recognized that government attorneys would often be unable to provide the attention necessary to litigate abortion cases properly, because they lacked either the time or the inclination to do so. The fund therefore began to consider the intervention strategy. It has used this tactic quite successfully in an area of major concern to anti-abortion groups—funding of abortions.

In addition to lobbying for consent provisions, immediately after *Roe* and *Doe* anti-abortion forces successfully convinced localities to restrict abortion services in publicly financed hospitals and states to limit Medicaid funds. As anticipated by Americans United for Life Legal Defense Fund, however, pro-choice forces filed suits against such funding restrictions almost as quickly as they were passed. As early as 1977 the United States Supreme Court decided three major cases, all of which dealt with states' or localities' restrictions on the use of funds. In all three the Court upheld the practice at issue.

While these cases were pending, however, Congress dealt pro-choice forces a major blow in 1976 when it passed a rider to the Labor-HEW Appropriations Act, known as the Hyde Amendment after its sponsor Henry Hyde. In its original form, the amendment stated: "None of the funds provided by this joint resolution shall be used to perform abortions except where the life of the mother would be endangered if the fetus were carried to full term." After the Hyde Amendment was originally passed by Congress, pro-choice groups immediately initiated *McRae v. Mathews* (1976) to challenge its constitutionality. At this time Hyde and several other members of Congress believed that HEW would be unable to "protect the interests of the unborn since HEW lobbied against the Hyde Amendment" (AUL Legal Defense Fund, 1976:3). Hyde, from Illinois, requested the Chicago-based AUL Legal Defense Fund to join in an effort to become intervenors to preserve the "adversary process."[5]

Americans United for Life Legal Defense Fund attorneys not only agreed to support Hyde as an intervenor but continued that support until 1980, when the Supreme Court finally ruled on the constitutionality of the amendment. Its brief seems to have been highly influential in the Court's opinion. AUL Legal Defense Fund attorneys, including Rosenblum, Horan, and Trueman, took great pains to rebut the legal arguments put forth by pro-choice forces, and also stressed that Congress was fully within its constitutional authority in enacting the legislation. Writing for the Court's majority, Justice Potter Stewart seemed to ground much of his opinion in this argument. "[We] cannot overturn duly enacted statutes simply because they may be unwise, improvident or out of harmony with a particular school of thought."

This decision, coupled with another funding case decided several weeks later — *Williams v. Zbaraz* (1980), in which the AUL Legal Defense Fund also acted as an intervenor — severely restricted the use of federal funds for abortions. In this case the Supreme Court addressed the question of whether an amendment to the Illinois Public Aid Code that prohibited funding of abortions "unless necessary for the preservation of the life of the woman" violated Title XIX of the Social Security Act. Once again representing AUL board member Dr. Diamond and another physician, AUL Legal Defense Fund attorneys intervened at the district court level and stayed with the case until the Supreme Court ruled in its favor in 1980. According to an Illinois state attorney, the fund's influence was "substantial and very active. They got in at the beginning and stayed with it" (Strobel, 1980). Given fears about the government's defense of the funding restrictions, AUL Legal Defense Fund attorneys may have played a critical role in securing the "favorable" decisions in this area.

AUL Legal Defense Fund attorneys take great pride in their victories in the funding and consent cases. However, in 1983 they suffered a severe setback. On 15 June 1983, the U.S. Supreme Court decided *Akron v. Akron Center for Reproductive Health*, which involved several local restrictions on abortions. The Court struck down each of the restrictions as unconstitutional intrusions upon a woman's right to obtain an abortion. This decision was a severe setback for both the AUL Legal Defense Fund and the entire anti-abortion move-ment. The organization had invested much time and money to assist attorneys for the sponsoring parties and to file briefs (Marzen, 1983). Yet the Court's majority opinion reflected what AUL Legal Defense Fund attorneys had learned earlier; the Court was simply unwill-ing to overturn *Roe* and *Doe*. Writing for the Court, Justice Lewis Powell specifically claimed that "the doctrine of *stare decisis*, while perhaps never entirely persuasive on a constitutional question, is a doctrine that demands respect in a society governed by the rule of law. We respect it today, and reaffirm *Roe v. Wade*."

The increasing professionalism of the fund's litigation efforts was evident even in this failure. Though rejecting its arguments in *Akron*, the majority opinion actually cited the fund's amicus curiae brief. It was the only interest group brief referred to in any of the opin-ions written in the case.

Evaluating the Assumptions:
Social Interest Groups

RESORT TO THE COURTS

The belief that interest groups will resort to the courts only when they are politically disadvantaged does not hold for conservative groups involved in social litigation. Several such groups, in fact, were highly successful in the legislative arena; Americans United for Life, along with other anti-abortion groups, stymied the efforts of liberal pro-choice groups to secure repeal of restrictive state abor-tion laws. Today's social groups took to the courts when they rec-ognized the significance and impact of court decisions, especially those of the U.S. Supreme Court. Americans for Effective Law En-forcement founders saw that *Miranda* and other liberal Warren Court decisions adversely affected criminal law and the enforce-ment process, and Americans United for Life watched its legislative victories evaporate by judicial fiat in 1973. And even though CDL was created before *Roth*, it took to the courts after it saw prosecu-tors lose convictions because of the Court's liberal interpretation of *Roth*.

Because all three groups recognized the importance of the judiciary, they were skeptical about allowing state prosecutors to defend their positions in court. In contrast to the conservative economic groups, social groups generally have government litigators on their side. But to varying degrees, the social groups viewed such primary support as insufficient, at best. Once they realized the potential significance of court decisions and the inadequacy of state or federal defense of their views, the groups chose to go to court themselves.

An additional factor explaining two of the groups' resort to the courts was "counterbalance." AELE founders, for example, specifically wanted to present the court with alternative positions to offset those presented by liberal groups. Similarly, Americans United for Life recognized the success pro-choice forces had achieved in court and so decided to mount opposition in the same arena.

Clearly, traditional assumptions about groups' reasons for litigating are of little use in explaining conservative social groups' decisions. These organizations go to court because they recognize the practical impact of judicial decisions and wish to have a hand in shaping them.

STRATEGIES

Scholars have generally agreed that interest groups prefer to sponsor cases directly. Although this appeared to be the preferred strategy of the early conservative social litigators, their modern counterparts have employed the full range of litigation strategies. All three groups first began to litigate as amicus curiae for basically the same reason: all generally side with government in litigation. Citizens for Decency through Law, for example, files amicus curiae briefs in cases where the government seeks to uphold obscenity convictions, while Americans United for Life Legal Defense Fund briefs reinforce government-sponsored abortion laws. All three groups initially felt compelled to utilize the amicus curiae strategy because governments generally represented their interests in court.

Only Americans for Effective Law Enforcement has continued to rely exclusively on the amicus curiae strategy. Its attorneys believe that the prosecution generally does a good job of presenting the narrow issues of the case and that their most useful role is to reinforce and to present the courts with the broader picture. Of course, under our system of criminal justice, governments are responsible for prosecution, but AELE could have opted for a special counsel or a cosponsor role. Instead, AELE leaders believe that, unlike the prosecution, they can take a long-term view of the litigation so as to avoid the creation of negative precedent and to help establish favorable legal principles. According to Carrington, "The Court, has, in effect, conceded that we are an informed source. We can bring in more empirical or intellectual data [than the parties]. We also bring in other cases to show prejudice" (Crawford, 1980: 33). Although AELE relies solely on the amicus curiae strategy, it does so with an eye toward building (and reducing) the laws governing the criminal justice system.

Unlike Americans for Effective Law Enforcement, Citizens for Decency through Law and the AUL Legal Defense Fund have been dissatisfied with the government's defense of their positions. To remedy deficiencies they perceive in government sponsorship of cases (or, in the case of CDL, at the request of government prosecutors), both have tried the intervention tactic. Although some legal scholars say this might not be the best strategy for groups that intend to assure their presence before the court (see Stern and Gressman, 1978), it has worked with some success for both groups. In *McRae*, despite opposition from U.S. attorneys, the AUL Legal Defense Fund intervened, and its brief was instrumental in the Court's ultimate resolution of the case.

Citizens for Decency through Law has also attempted to sponsor litigation. Because it currently employs several ex-prosecutors, with whom states are familiar, it has been allowed to represent the government in much the same way the National Consumers' League represented states in the early 1900s. Use of this tactic has allowed CDL to control the course of cases, which is viewed as particularly critical when the prosecution is poorly prepared.

Of the three social groups, only Americans for Effective Law Enforcement continues to rely exclusively on the amicus curiae strategy. Citizens for Decency through Law and Americans United for Life Legal Defense Fund, while continuing to file amicus curiae briefs, have moved away from that technique because they, like NCL, often find governments unable or unwilling to present their views adequately.

RESOURCES

Money. Whether participating as amici curiae, intervenors, or direct sponsors, groups require financial resources, although the amount of funding that is needed seems to vary with the strategy. To some extent, all three groups faced financial problems at the outset of their court efforts. Americans for Effective Law Enforcement was not financially stable until the early 1970s. Similarly, the AUL Legal Defense Fund's monetary support increased only after antiabortion groups recognized the need for legal defense of the limitations on *Roe* and *Doe* for which they lobbied, as the changes they sought were bound to be challenged by pro-choice groups.

One explanation for the financial difficulties of the groups during their formative years can be found in the timing of their formation or litigation. Because all turned to litigation to stop the further promulgation of adverse legal precedents, the environment in which they operated was inhospitable. As the political climate began to change during the 1970s, however, these groups became more financially secure.

AELE's financial status illustrates this phenomenon. During the mid-1960s, when many Americans were concerned with the rights of defendants, AELE was called a "hip-pocket" organization. During the Nixon presidency, however, AELE began to receive several sizable donations, including ones from Clement Stone and from the Scaife Foundation, which has also been a major supporter of conservative litigation. Since the early 1970s Scaife has provided yearly grants to AELE for operating funds and for its amicus curiae program. The grants have totaled between $100,000 and $200,000. Similarly, the Readers' Digest Foundation, beginning in 1967, has been the major supporter of CDL. Currently, Citizens for Decency through Law relies on private contributions, which total approximately $1 million per year (McCommon, 1983).

An additional explanation for the increasing financial success, at least of Citizens for Decency through Law and Americans for Effective Law Enforcement, was their retention of the services of Richard Viguerie. Between 1971 and 1972, one source claims, Viguerie raised approximately $2.3 million for CDL (Crawford, 1980:61–62). Several years later, in 1974, Viguerie also helped to raise money for AELE. Although Viguerie raised nearly $200,000 that year, he "took

90 percent of the contributions" for his own expenses (Crawford, 1980:66). AELE terminated its relationship with Viguerie because it found that it was "just trading dollars." It still uses the solicitation list created by Viguerie, however. AUL does not seem to have employed Viguerie, but it too has attempted a direct mail campaign of sorts to raise funds. Like the Equal Employment Advisory Council, AUL publishes numerous books, which it advertises through the mail. It uses the profits from these books and other pamphlets to further its interests.

All three groups started out without a solid financial backing. Thanks to the changed political climate in the United States and the attempts of the groups at direct mail solicitation and foundation support, all have been able to raise large amounts of money.

Government Support. Unlike the economic groups, which generally challenge government practices, conservative social groups have generally supported the government's position. Thus, the social groups' relationships with government tend to be more friendly than those of the economic groups.

Evidence of this cordial relationship comes from several sources. Most important, however, is that all three groups have had close outward ties with various individuals or administrations of the federal and state governments. Keating, for example, was Nixon's lone appointee to the Obscenity Commission. Because of his dissenting opinion from the majority report, Keating received a great deal of attention, which Citizens for Decency through Law used to its advantage. Because Keating's views were congruent with those of the Nixon administration, he received an important appointment that indirectly continues to serve CDL. Similarly, AELE received the Nixon administration's strong endorsement. That sort of support helped AELE to gain recognition and to raise money.

AELE also has close ties with the Reagan administration. In late 1979 Carrington and the AELE established the Victim's Rights Center of the AELE with the help of the current presidential adviser Edwin Meese, who was the "founding" director of the Center. The purposes of this now independent center, which has recently changed its name to Victims Assistance Legal Organization (VALOR), "are to promote and foster the legal rights of victims of crime and to utilize the legal system to prevent, where possible, future victimization" (VALOR, 1980–81:3; Duggan, 1982). In addition, AELE is one of a handful of organizations that regularly files amicus curiae briefs with state attorneys general. It has been able to develop such relationships because it often has the same objectives as the attorneys general and because it has gained the respect of law-enforcement officials, who regularly request AELE's participation (see Carrington, 1975).

In contrast, at least during the Carter years, the AUL Legal Defense Fund faced an administration inhospitable to its goals. Though Carter himself was against federal funding of abortions, HEW, under the leadership of Joseph Califano, promulgated an interpretation of the Hyde Amendment that was despised by anti-abortion groups (see Califano, 1981). But the AUL Legal Defense Fund at this time had several friends in Congress, including Hyde, who recognized the administration's adverse viewpoint and wanted to ensure that the anti-abortion position was well represented in court. They and the fund successfully intervened to present that view.

The fund's situation may have been reversed during the Reagan administration, however. Reagan has asked Congress to enact greater restrictions on abortions in the United States, thus helping the AUL Legal Defense Fund's position, but Congress has yet to pass such legislation or a constitutional amendment. If and when such legislation is passed under the Reagan administration, the fund may not be forced to intervene, because that administration is likely to defend its interests in court effectively. Evidence of the administration's support of AUL Legal Defense Fund goals came during the 1982 term of the Supreme Court, when Solicitor General Rex E. Lee argued orally as an amicus curiae in support of the city of Akron's restrictions on abortions.

Although the relations of social groups and the federal government vary depending on the administration in office, the three groups' government relationships can be generally characterized as cordial. Each has profited to some extent from its association with the federal government. Even when "hostile" administrations were in office, all three groups have maintained close ties at the state level. Americans for Effective Law Enforcement is the only group that regularly files amicus curiae briefs with state attorneys general, and both Citizens for Decency through Law and the AUL Legal Defense Fund file on behalf of the states.

Longevity. Greater resources have generally allowed all three groups to increase their use of litigation. Through continuous, increasing use of the courts, all the groups have attempted to build or to chip away at precedent, regardless of strategic choice. The AUL Legal Defense Fund, for example, has attempted to undercut *Roe* and *Doe* by reinforcing the legislative lobbying activities of anti-abortion forces through amicus curiae and intervenor briefs. Its initial briefs were too strident in tone, but it soon learned that one way to eradicate the 1973 decisions was through an "NAACP-type strategy"— the gradual, unrelenting, continuous, whittling away of negative precedent.

The litigation activities of Citizens for Decency through Law also reveal an upward trend. During the Warren Court era CDL participated in only nine United States Supreme Court cases, but since the appointment of Warren Burger to the Supreme Court its participation rate has more than doubled.

Americans for Effective Law Enforcement has also recognized the importance of increasing its use of the courts to chip away at the liberal Warren Court decisions. Inbau, in fact, has claimed that the law is "like a block of marble that eventually becomes a beautiful statue. You chip away bit-by-bit, until you carve the figure and features" (AELE, n.d., b). Support for Inbau's statement is found in AELE's increasing litigation activities. Between 1968 and 1970, for example, it participated in only three cases at the federal and state court levels; by 1980, its participation rate had tripled.

Because the conservative social groups were established or began litigating to combat unfavorable precedent, all are cognizant of the potential impact of judicial decisions. To avoid the creation of adverse precedent and, in fact, to create their own favorable principles, all three have attempted to increase their presence in court.

Staff. A fourth way in which interest groups have attempted to increase their effectiveness in litigation has been by recruiting experienced and committed staff. The three social groups bear several striking similarities. First, each was founded and initially led by one individual. Charles Keating not only founded Citizens for Decency through Law but continued to set its agenda. Similarly, Fred Inbau, the founder of Americans for Effective Law Enforcement, established the policies that continue to guide AELE's activity. Even the AUL Legal Defense Fund, which was created by several individuals, is still closely associated with Patrick Trueman, who is on Viguerie's list of "prominent" leaders of the "pro-family" movement (Viguerie, 1981:104).

All three groups are still very much associated with their founders. Nevertheless, all have made major personnel changes the past several years. Inbau continues to file amicus curiae briefs for Americans for Effective Law Enforcement, but has hired Frank Carrington to run the litigation program. There is some disagreement among other conservative groups over Carrington's expertise, but he too became a well-known figure during his tenure at AELE, writing several books, including *The Victims* (1975). Moreover, he is apparently well connected with the Reagan administration. In June 1980, for example, Meese asked Carrington to help establish three task forces dealing with crime. Carrington was subsequently placed as chair of one of those—the Crime Victim's Task Force (see VALOR, 1980–81). But in 1980 Carrington "left" AELE to help establish the Victims' Assistance Legal Organization (VALOR) in Virginia, which was initially affiliated with AELE but is now an independent because "it generated so much interest" (Duggan, 1982). When he left, Carrington "turned that position over to Wayne W. Schmidt," another AELE attorney and former law-enforcement official (Duggan, 1982; Carrington, 1975:246). But Carrington's name still appears on some AELE amicus curiae briefs when it jointly submits with VALOR.

Keating's Citizens for Decency through Law has taken a similar path. After Keating served on the Obscenity Commission, he sought to upgrade CDL's staff by hiring several former prosecutors, but his name is still found on CDL briefs. In sum, each organization has attempted to expand its staff and to retain attorneys well versed in their particular legal interests, but the imprints of their founders are still highly visible.

A third similarity between the three organizations is their use of outside counsel to supplement the work of staff attorneys. Almost immediately after each was formed or decided to use the courts, it set out to establish a network of cooperating attorneys. To some degree, all were successful in creating such a network. The AUL Legal Defense Fund, for example, continues to draw heavily on anti-abortion attorneys throughout the country.

The use of outside counsel has been helpful to the organizations in a number of ways. Because such counsel generally provides aid for no cost, the groups can save precious resources. In addition, all have attempted to draw on the talent of sympathetic attorneys throughout the United States because they view their particular legal interests as national in scope. The use of outside or "cooperating" counsel is imperative if they are to keep abreast of pending litigation throughout the nation.

A final, related similarity between two of the groups is that they have attempted to develop personnel ties with law schools, although each has gone about this task in a different way. The AUL Legal Defense Fund has used the more traditional internship route. In 1978 it established the David W. Louisdell Internship Program in honor of one of its founding members (AUL Legal Defense Fund, May 1978:6). Each year since that time, it has informed "every law school in the nation . . . of the summer long program" (AUL Legal Defense Fund, n.d., a) to attract the best students as interns and "to train future prolife lawyers" (AUL Legal Defense Fund, June 1979:4). Although its interns have been drawn from law schools as diverse as Pepperdine, Michigan, and Yale, all share one common trait: an ideological commitment to the anti-abortion movement. Many, in fact, were "long-time" activists with other anti-abortion groups before coming to the fund.

Americans for Effective Law Enforcement has also attempted to draw upon the nation's law school talent, but in a different way. It is proud of the fact that several of its staff members, including Inbau, Carrington, and Schmidt, have written "widely used" law school and college textbooks. Its now Independent Victim's Rights Center conducts seminars "in conjunction with various law schools" to examine criminal litigation (VALOR, 1980–81:6). Such activities have, of course, been facilitated by Professor Inbau's ties to the academic community. From the beginning Inbau relied on his colleagues to provide legal assistance to AELE.

Although Citizens for Decency through Law attorneys think an internship program might be "a nice thing," they have not yet developed one (McCommon, 1983). CDL runs short-term seminars throughout the United States for an audience it considers more important for the attainment of its overall goals: police and prosecutors. At these seminars CDL attempts to keep law-enforcement officials informed of the state of obscenity law generally, and of its activities and its availability for legal assistance (McCommon, 1983).

Publicity. All three organizations have recognized the importance of creating a favorable judicial climate through extra-judicial lobbying, but each has done its lobbying differently.

Soon after its creation Americans for Effective Law Enforcement sought greater visibility. Indeed, it had a head start, for even prior to its formation Inbau had written numerous law review articles presenting a law-and-order position. AELE continues to cite these articles in its briefs. AELE staff members and cooperating attorneys both have continued to inundate law reviews and write books on the limits of criminal rights, and the AELE has used these in formulating the legal arguments presented in its amicus curiae briefs.

Americans for Effective Law Enforcement has also backed up its position with statistical information. In *Opperman*, for example, it conducted a survey to reinforce its position, which Chief Justice Burger later used in his majority opinion. In short, AELE's public relations strategies — using publications and social science evidence — have resembled those used by liberal groups, including the NAACP Legal Defense Fund.

Americans United for Life Legal Defense Fund attorneys have also recognized the importance of extra-judicial lobbying outside the court, but their efforts have taken a different route. Like the Equal Employment Advisory Council, AUL Legal Defense Fund (and AUL) attorneys and sympathizers have endorsed or "produced scholarly and interesting examinations of the most important and controversial prolife issues" (AUL Legal Defense Fund, n.d., a). These publications, many of which cover both the legal and medical aspects of abortion, are often cited in AUL Legal Defense Fund briefs to bolster its legal position.

While relying less on law review articles and its own publications, Citizens for Decency through Law has used Keating's commission dissent as an extra-judicial lobbying device. In its amicus curiae in *Ferber*, for example, CDL noted:

> Charles Keating is the founder and co-counsel for Citizens for Decency through Law. . . . [He] was also a member of the Presidential Commission on Obscenity and Pornography. . . . [He] authored and released his findings . . . which explained the workings of the Commission and

the wealth of statistical information and human experience which prove
the relationship between the purveyance of obscenity to crimes and other
anti-social behavior. [CDL, October 1981:2–44]

Because of the publicity surrounding Keating's dissent, as well as
the Senate and the president's adoption of that opinion, the report
has been cited in several judicial opinions. This tactic may represent a nontraditional form of extra-judicial lobbying, but even so
it has brought attention and support for the objectives of the CDL.

Intergroup Support.   The early socially conservative litigators, like
current liberal groups, attempted to cooperate with one another
in litigation, but the current conservative social groups generally
have not done so. In fact only one — AELE — regularly cooperates
with other organizations by filing jointly submitted amicus curiae
briefs.

In the majority of its appearances before the Supreme Court
through the 1981 term, AELE has filed amicus curiae briefs with the
National District Attorneys Association (NDAA). Since its establishment in 1950, this group has regularly filed amicus curiae briefs
on its own behalf (Craemer, 1981), but now it rarely participates
without AELE. This relationship has been mutually beneficial; NDAA's
briefs have become more meaningful because of AELE attorneys' expertise and use of social science evidence, while NDAA support linked
AELE with a repeat-player in its first appearances before the Court.

In contrast, neither Citizens for Decency through Law nor the
AUL Legal Defense Fund regularly files briefs with other organizations, yet both cooperate with and receive financial support from
like-minded groups. Because of its status as the pro-life movement's
"only full-time" legal representative, the AUL Legal Defense Fund
enjoys the support of numerous anti-abortion groups. When asked
for material on its litigation efforts, National Right to Life, one of
the largest anti-abortion groups (see Merton, 1981), referred to its
association with AUL Legal Defense Fund. It added, "You may also
wish to contact Americans United for Life. . . . AUL is primarily a
legal defense fund for the prolife movement. . . . They also put
out an excellent newsletter dealing with litigation" (Moore, 1981).

Similarly, Citizens for Decency through Law representatives continue to speak before community organizations, to garner support
for their cause. Since its inception, CDL members have allegedly had

ties with several other conservative organizations, including the John Birch Society (*Group Research,* 28 January 1974:2).

SUCCESS

Once again, three indicators are used to measure success. The first — overall attainment of litigation goals — shows mixed success for the conservative social groups. Citizens for Decency through Law has had some effect on expanding the definition of obscenity. In one of its most recent cases, *Ferber,* CDL's argument, which suggested that child pornography is by its very nature obscene, was adopted by the Court. Similarly, Americans for Effective Law Enforcement has helped to undermine the liberal Warren Court revolution, particularly in the area of search and seizure. AELE would like to see the ultimate eradication of the exclusionary rule, and it has made progress toward this objective through the amicus curiae brief strategy. Since the Court's decision in *Ross,* for example, which relied on arguments presented by AELE, almost all evidence obtained from car searches without warrants can be admitted in court. The AUL Legal Defense Fund, whose ultimate objective is to overturn *Roe* and *Doe,* has also made some progress. Initially, it was impatient; it wanted the Court to overrule its 1973 decisions immediately. But over time it has learned that by whittling away at those decisions through funding and consent restrictions it could severely limit *Roe's* impact.

As indicated in table 4-1, all three groups score relatively high on the second measure of success, percentage of cases won — at least when compared with the economic litigators. Through the 1981 term of the Burger Court, all three organizations won more than 50 percent of their cases. As with the three economic groups, however, such figures may be misleading. Although there may be some correspondence between their growing expertise and attainment of a repeat-player status and success rates, their success is also due to the increasing conservatism of the Burger Court, at least in these areas of the law. During its 1970 through 1981 terms, for example, the Supreme Court decided half of the sixteen reproductive freedom cases in favor of the anti-abortion position. Similarly, AELE's high success rate and CDL's rising rate can, at least in part, be attributed to the Burger Court's pro-law-and-order and anti-obscenity

Table 4-1
Success Rates of Social Litigators

	Warren Court		Burger Court*	
	% cases won**	total cases***	% cases won	total cases
CDL	0%	9	55%	18
AELE	100%	1	61%	36
AULLDF	–	–	57%	7

Note: Data compiled by author.
*Includes the 1969 through 1981 terms of the Court.
**Calculated on the basis of whether the Court adopted the position advocated by the group.
***Total U.S. Supreme Court cases in which the group had been involved from the year it began litigating through the 1981 term of the Court.

postures. According to Richard Funston, "except in the areas of criminal law and the censorship of obscenity, the work of the Warren Court remains intact" (Funston, 1977).

On the final measure of success — assessments of group activities by the groups and regular opponents — the social groups also rate high. The groups themselves believe that they have made some progress toward the attainment of their objectives, and some of their regular opponents voiced similar views. According to one ACLU attorney who regularly faced the AUL Legal Defense Fund in court:

> At the outset, they used tremendously inflammatory rhetoric, out of court and in their briefs, and there was a sad lack of knowledge of federal procedure.
> But now there's professionalism. Their briefs are smoother; they don't have that hysterical tone to them. Their arguments were nowhere near the exotic kind they've used in other law suits. [Strobel, 1980]

ACLU officials have been more critical of Americans for Effective Law Enforcement. Though they have not necessarily criticized the quality of its work, they have charged that AELE "has a predilection, which . . . is fair to call a bias, in favor of police — if the police are doing it, it must be right and legal. *And if it isn't legal, then certainly right*" (Crawford, 1980:109; emphasis added). Ill feeling between these two organizations are to be expected, given that their goals are diametrically opposed. Carrington, for example, has claimed:

> In its supreme lack of concern for the rights of the law-abiding, the ACLU has evidenced a totally antivictim attitude. This can be illustrated by the fact that the Exclusionary Rule and the *Miranda* decision have resulted in as much or more victimization of innocent individuals as any two court decisions in our history. The ACLU, *of course*, thoroughly supports both. [Carrington, 1975:202–3; emphasis added]

Yet despite mutual criticisms, there appears as well to be a mutual respect among the social groups and their opponents. Many of the social groups were formed in response to the success of their liberal counterparts, and liberal groups now recognize that their presentations in the areas of criminal rights, obscenity, and abortion will no longer go unchallenged. In fact, it is evident that the quality of conservative opposition has increased over time and that liberal groups recognize this, too.

This chapter has revealed several differences between liberal and conservative social groups. First, the idea that political disadvantage explains conservative social groups' resort to the courts has little utility. These groups do not view their goals as unobtainable in the legislative, executive, or electoral arenas, but they do recognize the significance of judicial decisions, and so they turn to litigation. Second, while all three social groups are concerned with building (or chipping away at) precedent, they have employed the range of litigation strategies. Yet, like some liberal groups, two of the social groups moved away from sole reliance on the amicus curiae brief after they found their views inadequately represented by state or federal attorneys. Finally, even though the social groups have utilized most of the resources interest groups usually depend on, they have employed them somewhat otherwise than liberal groups. Like current conservative economic groups, most social litigators tend to cooperate with other groups *outside* of the courtroom. And, though they have attempted to recruit expert legal counsel, all three continue to be associated with one or two individuals.

5 CONSERVATIVE PUBLIC INTEREST LITIGATION SINCE THE 1970s

During the late 1930s the American Liberty League created the National Lawyers' Committee to render legal advice and to challenge New Deal legislation through litigation. Though the committee existed for only five years, it was an important early conservative litigator. It recruited the best attorneys of the day, and it acted on the basis of a coherent ideology: that the public interest was best served when government avoided needless entanglement with its constituents.

The National Lawyers' Committee disbanded in 1940. Thirty years later, a new breed of conservative public interest law firm emerged to espouse a similar ideology in court. These new groups differ from the Lawyers' Committee in two ways. First, they emerged in response not to the passage of federal aid legislation, but to the rise of a redistributive movement — the liberal public interest law movement. Second, there exists not one conservative public interest law firm but several. They are located throughout the United States, forming a network of conservative public interest groups.

Because of the unusual character of the history and structure of the conservative interest groups that center their activities in public interest issues, before examining traditional assumptions this chapter first traces the salient facts of the movement's historical background.

The Growth of Liberal Public Interest Law

The 1960s comprised a turbulent era in U.S. history, as many protested, peaceably and militantly, against racism, the draft, and the Vietnam War, and more generally against government. Others turned to the courts in the belief that they could not reach their goals in traditional political arenas. According to one source, the late 1960s and early 1970s "was a time of great proliferation and growth for public interest law" (Council for Public Interest Law, 1976:57). Over this ten-year period several different strains of liberal public interest law firms developed almost simultaneously.

The first phase can be dated from the publication in 1963 of Ralph Nader's *Unsafe at Any Speed*, which detailed the problems inherent in General Motor's design and manufacture of its Corvair. The book immediately thrust its author into the national spotlight. Nader became a symbol of the consumer movement; his speeches and television appearances furthered his image as "the" representative of citizens before government (see Handler, 1978a; de Toledano, 1975).

Within two years of publication of his book, Nader began to establish what has been termed the "Nader Network" (Burt, 1982). In 1967 he established the Center for the Study of Responsive Law, which was shortly followed by creation of the Public Interest Research Group (PIRG), a consumer-oriented public interest law firm (see Handler, 1978a; Snow and Weisbrod, 1978). Since the creation of PIRG the Nader network has grown tremendously (see Burt, 1982). One source currently estimates the network to include over twenty diverse groups (Dye and Zeigler, 1983:235).

Nader was not only the catalyst for the creation of the first kind of liberal public interest law firm, he also played a role in developing the second, which began with the creation of the Center for Law and Social Policy (CLASP) in 1969. CLASP was officially founded by Charles Halpern, former clerk at the District of Columbia Court of Appeals (see Broder, 1980; Halpern and Cunningham, 1971), but Nader assisted with its planning (Council for Public Interest Law, 1976:63). CLASP differed significantly from the Nader organizations. Instead of specializing in a particular area of the law, it handled a variety of cases, ranging from environmental protection to media law.

This form of liberal public interest law became the prototype for firms during the second phase of the decade. Numerous groups, including Public Advocates and the Center for Law in the Public Interest, were established to bring their view of the public interest to the judicial arena. Their strategies and tactics, like those of the Nader groups, closely resembled those used by the early liberal interest group litigators: they sponsored cases, they were staffed by young, well-educated attorneys, and they cooperated with each other. This resemblance was not coincidental. The public interest law firms recognized the success of their predecessors, including the NAACP Legal Defense Fund and the American Civil Liberties Union, and sought to emulate their tactics.

By the mid-1970s more than seventy groups were active and their impact on the law was clear. According to some observers, the success of the liberal public interest law movement is apparent in two ways. First, liberal public interest law firms successfully used the courts to carve out areas of the law that did not previously exist (see Horowitz, 1980:11; Momboisse, 1980a:14; Council for Public Interest Law, 1976; Weisbrod, ed., 1978). Consumer and environmental law and gender-based discrimination are but a few of the examples analysts use to illustrate this point. A second, and perhaps more significant, achievement of the new liberal public interest law movement is that since the early 1970s, the term "public interest," at least as employed in judicial circles, has become identified with the defense of liberal interests (see Council for Public Interest Law, 1976; Handler, 1978a; Ford, 1973). According to one observer of public interest law, "traditional public interest firms have created a near-identity in their legal ideology because of their self-asserted title and their almost uniform bias in favor of the enhancement of governmental largely federal power" (Horowitz, 1980:8).

The First Conservative Response:
The Pacific Legal Foundation

As early as 1972 some conservatives began to see that they needed to bring their definition of the public interest to court. The new awareness first took concrete form in California, where then governor Ronald Reagan was attempting to secure passage of welfare reforms. Reagan faced opposition not only in the state house but, once the reforms were enacted, in court, where several politically "disadvantaged" liberal interest groups challenged the new laws. During both the legislative and litigative battles two members of the Reagan administration — Ronald Zumbrun, an advisor to the department of welfare who had lobbied for the reforms, and Raymond Momboisse, an assistant attorney general who had litigated on behalf of the administration — realized that conservative interests were being adversely affected when liberal public interest law firms went to court, claiming that they alone represented "the" public interest. According to Momboisse, "the state was at a tremendous disadvantage [because] the opposition had the ability to throw tremendous manpower into the litigation" (Broder, 1980:251).

Based on their common experience with liberal interest groups, Zumbrun and Momboisse, along with members of an advisory committee of the California State Chamber of Commerce and Reagan staffers, including Edwin Meese, began to explore the possibility of creating a conservative public interest law firm in the image of liberal groups, a new group that would provide the courts with another view of the public interest. Like their predecessors who had formed the National Lawyers' Committee, these conservatives wanted to establish an organization that would have as its guiding tenet the eradication of the "needless" government regulation so desired by liberal groups.

The result of this "exploration" was the establishment of the Pacific Legal Foundation (PLF) in Sacramento, California, in 1973. As originally envisioned by its founders, the PLF was to be a small firm staffed by two attorneys, Zumbrun and Momboisse, and managed by a fifteen-member board of directors originally composed of the Advisory Committee of the state Chamber of Commerce (Singer, 1979). The Advisory Committee specifically recommended that the PLF be independent and not a legal arm of the state chamber of commerce. Its founders believed that the PLF would handle legal issues rather than advocate specific causes arising in California and dealing with the environment, in particular.

Within a year of its establishment, however, the Pacific Legal Foundation saw that to be effective, it had to expand its staff and change its locale. The case that prompted the decision involved the

Trident submarine: the PLF opposed several liberal groups that were fighting its development. The opposition, knowing the organization would have problems litigating in Washington, D.C., where the case was being tried, used the PLF's California locale to its own advantage in several procedural manipulations (Momboisse, 1982). In response to this experience, Momboisse opened an affiliate PLF office in the nation's capital in 1974.

At first the Pacific Legal Foundation had trouble obtaining adequate funding to run both offices. According to Horowitz, it underwent "three years of financial insecurity, during the first two years of which no foundation grants were received" (Horowitz, 1980:34). But like other earlier conservative interest group litigators, the PLF attracted funds as it became more visible and successful in court. During its early years it participated as amicus in litigation involving a variety of issues, while retaining a particular interest in environmental litigation. Through these amicus curiae briefs and by sporadically sponsoring cases, the PLF gained recognition that focused on its uniqueness: it was the only group at the time to attempt to bring a different definition of the public interest to court. Because it was "needed and wanted" (Momboisse, 1980a:41), the PLF began to receive sizable contributions from individuals, businesses, associations, and foundations, including the Scaife family, the Olin and Hearst foundations, and the Lilly Endowment. Increased funding in turn led to major expansion. As the organization hired more attorneys, it expanded its case load. By 1982 PLF had eighteen full-time attorneys and was involved in more than one hundred cases.

The Pacific Legal Foundation has expanded beyond the original intent of its founders, but it has remained true to their original objective: to represent one version of the public interest in a variety of issue areas. Because of its concern with "issues" rather than with "causes," the PLF claims to have approached litigation in a markedly different way from that of its liberal opponents. During the PLF's formative years, for example, Momboisse criticized liberal public interest law firms for "creating cases" (Momboisse, 1980a). Thus, while increased funding has allowed the PLF to sponsor more cases, which after years of filing amicus curiae briefs is now its preferred tactic, it has not attempted to bring test cases to court.[1] Rather, PLF attorneys "have been involved in systematic [litigation] campaigns . . . from the other side" (Momboisse, 1982) by putting liberal groups on the defensive. In *Weinberger v. Catholic Action Peace Education Project of Hawaii* (1981), for example, a liberal group filed a suit to stop the United States government from building a weapons storage facility in Hawaii. The firm argued that the navy had failed to indicate on its environmental impact statement whether nuclear weapons would be stored in the facility. In supporting the U.S. Navy's position, the PLF turned the suit around by placing the environmental group on the defensive. Instead of addressing the omission in the impact statement, the PLF argued that the navy should not be required to disclose possible "national defense secrets" in its statements. In 1981 the U.S. Supreme Court adopted the PLF's arguments, noting:

> Since the public disclosure requirements of NEPA [the National Environmental Protection Act] are governed by FOIA [the Freedom of Information Act], it is clear that Congress intended that the public's interest in ensuring that federal agencies comply with NEPA must give way to the Government's need to preserve military secrets. In the instant case, an EIS [Environmental Impact Statement] concerning a proposal to store nuclear weapons . . . is classified information exempt from disclosure to the public. [454 U.S. at 145–46]

Beyond this supposed difference in strategy, however, the Pacific Legal Foundation resembles its liberal counterparts in a number of significant ways. Like many successful liberal groups, the PLF has established a stringent case selection procedure. Cases are initially assigned to one attorney to investigate. Once that attorney prepares a two-page summary of the case, including a description of the question of public interest law, the case is reviewed by the entire legal staff in Sacramento and in the District of Columbia. An opinion is then given to an eighteen-member board of directors, at least half of whom are attorneys, for a final decision. This procedure eliminates twenty-nine of every thirty cases that come to the organization for review (Wood, 1981).

Both liberal public interest law firms and the Pacific Legal Foundation attempt to cooperate with government officials. From the beginning, PLF founders were associated with government; both Momboisse and Zumbrun worked for Governor Reagan. Moreover, in its first court appearance PLF attorneys provided legal assistance to the U.S. Department of Forestry, which had asked for their help.

Momboisse has claimed that access was "impossible" during the Carter administration, but the situation has changed markedly since 1980. According to Momboisse, Reagan's interest in reforming the bureaucracy and lessening government's influence in the private sector are consistent with policies favored by the Pacific Legal Foundation. But as Momboisse also noted, full cooperation is difficult because, although the president may be interested in reform, bureaucratic regulators are not. Consequently, PLF is still often placed in the position of having to challenge government practices (Momboisse, 1982).

Liberal public interest law firms and the Pacific Legal Foundation both recruit and train expert attorneys. Although conservative groups generally, and the PLF in particular, have been criticized for their failure to recruit conservative ideologues from Ivy League law schools (see Horowitz, 1980; 1981; Kristol, 1981), the PLF has actively attempted to "train outstanding law school graduates" through its College of Public Interest Law, which was established in 1979 (PLF, 1979–80:12). In this program, the young attorneys intern for one to two years to learn the intricacies of the PLF version of the public interest. The PLF also attempts to insure the selection of outstanding individuals by placing the college under the direction of a board of directors made up predominantly of law school professors from well-known California institutions like Stanford and UCLA (PLF, 1981–82:12). Like its liberal counterparts, PLF recognizes the importance of injecting new blood into the organization.

Finally, the Pacific Legal Foundation resembles liberal groups in its cooperation with other firms. PLF leaders were instrumental in the establishment of another conservative public interest law firm, the Mountain States Legal Foundation (Momboisse, 1982). And its staff members regularly attend the Heritage Foundation legal luncheons. Although the PLF has outward ties with some other groups, like its conservative predecessors and the current economic groups it generally avoids cooperation in litigation. The PLF has "seldom gone into litigation that other public interest law firms are doing because there's only a limited amount of manpower . . . when the same view is being presented" (Momboisse, 1982). Like the economic litigators, then, the PLF follows the deliberate noncooperation tactic to avoid needless duplication of effort.

Since its creation the Pacific Legal Foundation has combined the tactics of liberal public interest law firms with those it believes complement its own "unique" purpose and ideology. Use of this combination of tactics, coupled with the fact that the PLF was the first conservative public interest law firm, has prompted one founder to declare that, unlike the National Lawyers' Committee, "the PLF is here to stay; for it is the new wave of public interest law" (Momboisse, 1980b).

The National Legal Center for the Public Interest

When the Pacific Legal Foundation was establishing itself as a counterbalance to liberal public interest law firms in California during the early 1970s, it began to consider the need for an expanded conservative public interest law movement. To build a broader base, besides opening its D.C. office the PLF commissioned Leonard Theberge, a former Federal Power Commission and U.S. attorney, to conduct a study on the need for more conservative public interest law centers in the United States.

Theberge's study indicated that, given what he termed the "immediate success" of the Pacific Legal Foundation, more regional grass-roots centers should be created in its image to bring the conservative definition of the public interest to court. Before PLF leaders could consider the advisability of such a plan, Theberge, assisted by a $200,000 start-up grant from the Scaife Foundation, established the National Legal Center for the Public Interest (NLCPI) in 1975, with the sole purpose of establishing a network of conservative public interest law firms throughout the United States (Singer, 1979).

Theberge traveled throughout the United States presenting information to "leading citizens," particularly businessmen and women, on the dangers of liberal public interest law and on the need for conservative counterbalances in court (Hueter, 1982). Within one year he was able to recruit several prominent conservatives who were instrumental in the subsequent establishment of three foundations — the Southeastern Legal Foundation, in Atlanta; the Mid-America Legal Foundation, in Chicago; and the Great Plains Legal Foundation in Kansas City, Missouri.[2] By 1978 the National Legal Center, under the leadership of Theberge, had facilitated the creation of three other affiliated firms: Mountain States, in Denver; the Mid-Atlantic, in Philadelphia; and the Capital Legal Foundation, in Washington, D.C.

It is beyond the scope of this book to examine all these affiliates in detail, but a few words about their development are in order. In attempting to establish regional centers, Theberge not only sought out citizens who agreed with his ideology, but also attempted to find well-known conservatives, generally businesspeople, to run each firm. Ben Blackburn, a former member of Congress, became the first president of the Southeastern Legal Foundation. James Watt, later secretary of the interior under Reagan, held a similar position at the Mountain States Legal Foundation (MSLF). Christopher Bond, a former governor of Missouri and head of the Chamber of Commerce of the United States, was the first president of the Great Plains Legal Foundation.

Theberge also attempted to establish firms that would remain regional. Each of the six affiliated firms was therefore charged with guarding the interests of a specified geographical area by litigating issues of regional concern. While some firms, most notably the Capital Legal Foundation, have veered off from Theberge's original plan, most have continued to concentrate on regional concerns. The Mountain States Legal Foundation, for example, is most concerned with land use and other more general environmental issues west of the "100th meridian."

Most of these affiliated foundations, established by prominent conservatives to guard the conservative public interest in various regions, have not grown as fast as the Pacific Legal Foundation. Only the Mountain States Legal Foundation, which no longer considers itself dependent upon the National Legal Center, has more than five attorneys and receives more than $1.5 million in funding (Mellor, 1982). The Southeastern Legal Foundation, though its contributors consist mostly of business interests, is operating on a budget far smaller than that of the MSLF or of the unaffiliated PLF, and has only five attorneys.

According to some insiders, this lack of growth has occurred for the same reason that the National Chamber Litigation Center has stagnated: use of the amicus curiae strategy to appease business members, rather than to bring a new ideology to court. The Southeastern Legal Foundation, for example, has relied almost exclusively on participation as amicus curiae, and in far fewer cases per year than the PLF or the MSLF. Its 1981 docket lists five cases, in most of which it has supported claims being advanced by business interests.

Another reason for the lack of growth of the affiliated centers was Theberge's recruitment of business-oriented persons, rather than expert attorneys, to top positions. One observer of conservative public interest law has claimed: "That businessmen are the people who create the productive economy which makes much of American life possible need not be disputed. Yet it is an irony, unhappy but true, that the very practical skills which make businessmen effective as such probably serve as handicaps in the ideological-intellectual battlegrounds in which conservative public interest law firms must do their work" (Horowitz, 1980:71). Because of many of the conservative public interest law firms' preoccupation with keeping businesses happy by relying on the amicus curiae and on individuals from the world of business, some have called them "business-oriented legal foundations" instead of conservative public interest law firms (see Jordan and Rubin, 1981; Cass and Goetz, n.d.).

Others, however, blame the National Legal Center for the inability of the regional organizations to function as well as the Pacific Legal Foundation (Momboisse, 1982; Johnson, 1983; Popeo, 1983). Since establishment of these firms, the NLCPI has been the center of a great deal of controversy, from numerous sources. In its reports and in interviews, the NLCPI claims to act as a "clearinghouse" for member firms. Its president, Ernest B. Hueter, a former bakery executive from Kansas who was typical of Theberge's original recruits, has stated that NLCPI helps to identify potentially good cases, provides research services, and files cases in the District of Columbia for its member firms. Hueter characterized the relationship between NLCPI and the regionals as "very close" (Hueter, 1982). Attorneys in both affiliated and nonaffiliated firms, however, have strongly disagreed with Hueter's assessment. One foundation attorney claimed that how much help the National Legal Center actually provided was "questionable." He also noted that all the firms established by the NLCPI were actually quite independent, even though the NLCPI had "theoretically" helped to get them started. Others are embarrassed to admit any connection with the National Legal Center, viewing it as a superfluous organization.

Such problems between the NLCPI and the legal foundations

prompted the Heritage Foundation to become involved with the conservative public interest law network in 1977. Willa Johnson, then a new staffer at Heritage, recognized that the various foundations had "compatible goals" but were not communicating (Johnson, 1983). Heritage stepped in to fill the role that the NLCPI was designed to play; it attempted to act as a coordinator for the conservative public interest law movement, believing that this role was critical to the survival of the movement, but recognizing that the NLCPI could not act as a facilitator. The NLCPI still was distrusted by the Pacific Legal Foundation, which was against its establishment from the beginning and was viewed by other firms as competing for funds. In contrast, the Heritage Foundation's intervention was welcomed by the PLF, which viewed it as a neutral party.

To get the firms to "start talking," Heritage began to hold monthly luncheons. Regulars at the luncheons include representatives from the local conservative public interest law firms and other conservative interest groups, including National Right to Work and the National Chamber Litigation Center. The intellectual quality of the luncheons varies depending on which representatives the organizations choose to send and on the "mood" of the individuals present, a Heritage representative says, but these occasions have generally helped develop a cohesive conservative network (Johnson, 1983). A conservative public interest law attorney remarked that the luncheons help "keep people civilized."

While these luncheons help the conservative public interest law movement in a general way, they have not helped the National Legal Center's image; they have merely lent credence to the notion that the center is inept as a coordinating organization. The NLCPI's problem was exacerbated in 1980 when it was severely criticized in the so-called Horowitz Report.

In the late 1970's Michael Horowitz, who is currently the chief legal advisor of the Office of Management and Budget, was commissioned by the Scaife Foundation to assess the state of conservative public interest law (Horowitz, 1983). After some investigation Horowitz issued his report in 1980. "NLCPI is of no present value. Unless radically altered in board membership and concept, it is never likely to be," the report stated bluntly. "Although NLCPI speaks vaguely of its 'coordinative and supportive' role vis-a-vis its six constituent firms, it has in fact done and is capable of doing little or nothing . . . given its lack of utility or meaning to successful firms and its lack of impact on or ability to critique the work of its unsuccessful firms" (1980:48–50).

Horowitz based his conclusions about the National Legal Center on several factors,[3] the most important of which was that, instead of helping member firms raise money after their establishment, the center actually competed with them for financial support. As other evaluators of interest group litigation have indicated (see O'Connor, 1980; Berger, 1979), competition among like-minded groups for limited resources can be devastating to the creation of a concentrated litigation strategy. One of the NLCPI's affiliated firms, the Capital Legal Foundation, actually broke with the center over a funding dispute (Kimball, 1982).

NLCPI officials hesitate to discuss the Horowitz Report except to point out that most of his information was secondhand (Hueter, 1982). Other firms reluctantly admit that Horowitz's criticisms of the NLCPI, though harsh, were "justified." Since publication of the report the NLCPI has attempted to expand its activities. It currently publishes monographs by well-known conservatives in specific areas of interest and is exploring the possibility of launching a law review at Harvard University. But instead of working to its advantage these changes have only underscored the notion that the center cannot find its niche in the conservative public interest law movement; some say it "changes direction once a week." Many of those involved in the conservative public interest law movement are doubtful of the NLCPI's future viability. One individual who is intimately involved in the movement voiced the general sentiment: "They've outlived their purpose . . . [and] might as well shut down."

The Washington Legal Foundation: An Unaffiliated Foundation

While the National Legal Center was establishing a regional network of litigating firms, others were forming independent conservative public interest law firms. During the 1970s several firms not affiliated with the NLCPI were established.[4] But to date most people involved in the movement claim that only one, the Washington Legal

Foundation (WLF), has made a sizable impact on conservative public interest law.

To a large extent, the Washington Legal Foundation's effectiveness is due to the efforts of its founder, Dan Popeo. Popeo, who has been called the "Nader of the Right" (see Brophy, 1980; Whitney, 1982),[5] recognized the need for a conservative legal foundation while working for the Nixon administration. After graduating from Georgetown Law School in 1975, Popeo took a position on the White House legal staff. While he "molded friendships" during this period, he saw the inability of government to work out policy problems. This view was only reinforced when he left the White House to take a position as a trial attorney in the Department of the Interior. There, he concluded that the bureaucracy not only had too much power but was insensitive to the needs of business (Popeo, 1983). Like Zumbrun and Momboisse, Popeo blamed these deficiencies on the liberal public interest law movement generally and on the Nader groups in particular. The Nader solution of "more government," he claimed, had created many unnecessary and "arbitrary" regulations (Whitney, 1982).

Based on his dissatisfaction with the Nader-influenced bureaucracy, Popeo took out a $15,000 loan in 1976 to establish the Washington Legal Foundation, which became functional in 1977 (Popeo, 1983). Explaining the need for such an organization, he said:

> As Conservatives, we saw the need for an organization that would devote legal resources to cases that relate to government regulations, rights for the victims of crime, and the civil liberties of small businessmen; one that would defend the principles of Free Enterprise and constitutional law in dealings with the governmental agencies and the courts. So we formed the WLF.   [quoted in Rees, 1982]

Popeo knew about the affiliated network of conservative public interest law firms that Theberge was in the process of creating, but he chose not to "affiliate"[6] for two reasons. First, Popeo wanted the Washington Legal Foundation to be a membership-based firm, and felt it would be contradictory to call the WLF a public interest law firm if it was not supported by the public. To marshal the kind of support he sought Popeo retained the services of Richard Viguerie. According to Popeo, the results of Viguerie's efforts were remarkable; the WLF currently has more than 85,000 members and a budget of $1.5 million, he claims, making it among the largest conservative public interest law firms. Although Popeo still uses direct mail fund raising, he later "parted ways" with Viguerie because of the cost of retaining his services and because Viguerie was "too individualistic" (Popeo, 1983). A second reason Popeo wanted to remain unaffiliated was that he thought the wlf should be national rather than regional in scope. His interest in maintaining a national outlook explains why he decided to establish headquarters in the District of Columbia (Popeo, 1983). In 1982, however, the wlf opened its first affiliate office in Dallas, Texas. According to Popeo, the wlf will continue to expand as long as there is sufficient interest.

Popeo's emphasis on "the public" and on national interests has led him to select cases for the Washington Legal Foundation's participation that both underscore the conservative ideology and bring publicity to the organization. In its first case the wlf represented sixty-one members of Congress in their suit against what it called President Carter's "transfer" of the Panama Canal. Because of the wlf's work in this case, several years later Senator Barry Goldwater called on Popeo to represent him in a similar suit, *Goldwater v. Carter* 1979), in which the wlf argued that Carter's termination of the Taiwan treaty was unconstitutional because he had failed to consult the Senate. Although these cases were not planned as part of a litigation strategy, they helped the wlf to solidify its reputation within the conservative community in the capital.

Favorable publicity has also come through the Washington Legal Foundation's involvement in a variety of issue areas that are of little concern to the affiliated conservative public interest law firms. For example, the rights of crime victims constitute an issue having top priority. wlf has always had some interest in this area, believing that the defense of victims is a logical extension of its free-enterprise philosophy, but most of the attention it has received has focused on its conduct of the *McCarthy* suit. Timothy McCarthy, the secret service agent who was shot in John Hinckley's attempted assassination of President Reagan, called the wlf on the advice of "friends in the White House" who knew of Popeo's work. The wlf has initiated a civil suit against Hinckley on McCarthy's behalf.

Through direct sponsorship of highly salient cases, including *Goldwater* and *McCarthy*, Popeo has solidified his reputation as the "Nader of the Right." But unlike the Pacific Legal Foundation, which claims it is averse to participation as amicus curiae, the Washington Legal Foundation has no "conscious policy to avoid" that strategy (Popeo, 1983). Popeo is proud of the fact that although he has filed amicus curiae briefs in a variety of cases, the WLF has been denied participation only once.

The Washington Legal Foundation's reason for using the amicus curiae in some cases is analogous to that of Americans for Effective Law Enforcement; WLF often files to counterbalance the claims of liberal groups when it cannot actually sponsor a particular case. In its 1982 annual report, the WLF described its amicus curiae participation in *Eddings v. Oklahoma* (1982): "WLF supports State of Oklahoma's capital punishment law in Supreme Court against challenge by NAACP Legal Defense Fund attorneys defending a youth who killed a police officer with a sawed-off shot gun" (WLF, 1982a:6).

Thus, to some extent, the Washington Legal Foundation is dissimilar to the Pacific Legal Foundation and to several of the firms established by Theberge in its image. But the WLF resembles the other conservative public interest law firms in at least three significant ways. First, as exemplified by its participation in a range of cases, WLF does not consciously pursue a test-case strategy. According to Popeo, who makes the litigation decisions for the firm, every case must be judged on its own merits, and not as part of a series (Popeo, 1983). Avoidance of a test-case strategy does not necessarily mean a lack of interest in the creation of favorable precedent. One of the reasons Popeo took *McCarthy* was to help build new precedent to encourage "crime victims around the United States to bring suits in the interest of justice" (quoted in Rees, 1982).

Second, the Washington Legal Foundation's view of the public interest resembles that of the regional counterparts. While Popeo is considered by some in the movement to be more "new right" than most, his views are quite like those of other conservative public interest law firm attorneys. According to Popeo, the WLF has one "overriding goal: to balance the public interest by addressing concerns of mainstream Americans tired of too much government, too many taxes, too much crime, and too few opportunities to make important decisions without governmental interference" (WLF, 1982a:4).

Finally, the Washington Legal Foundation has begun recently to recognize the need to recruit expert attorneys and to develop "ties with local and national colleges, universities and law schools" (WLF,

1982a:5). This task was facilitated by the establishment of the WLF College Intern Program, in which students assist WLF attorneys and staffers in the District of Columbia. Popeo claims that he has done little recruitment either for staff attorneys or for interns, because good talent has sought him out. A former intern substantiates Popeo's claim:

> Throughout my first year of law school, I delighted in telling classmates that my plans included pursuing public interest law. And they immediately understood. I was going to defend indigent criminals, horsewhip businesses through government regulation. . . . I savored the benedictory gleam in their eyes . . . before explaining that I had other malefactors in mind . . . [but] I didn't know where I was going to practice the kind of public interest law I had in mind (were there such places?) until I discovered and went to work for the Washington Legal Foundation. [Charen, 1982]

The WLF may have taken a different tack from the other firms, but it is perceived by those involved to be an integral part of the conservative public interest law movement in the United States.

Evaluating the Assumptions: Conservative Public Interest Law Firms

RESORT TO THE COURTS

Scholars have assumed that most interest groups, including liberal public interest law firms that emerged during the late 1960s and early 1970s, resorted to litigation because they could not obtain rights in other political forums. The explanation suits the case of many liberal groups, but it does not accurately describe conservative public interest law firm activity.

Many founders of conservative public interest law firms, individuals like Momboisse and Zumbrun, were well connected in government and thus had ready access to high officials. These men formed conservative public interest law firms, not because they were disadvantaged in the legislative or executive arenas, but because they viewed conservatives as disadvantaged in the courts, where they believed that liberal firms had a "moral monopoly" on the public interest.

To some extent, there are close parallels here with the rise of economic litigators. In contrast to the economic groups, however, some conservative public interest law firms claim to be more concerned with the "war of ideologies" than with business interests; they have attempted to bring their view of the public interest to court to end the liberal monopoly. And although their view of the public interest at times necessarily coincides with that of business, conservative public interest law firm leaders claim that business is not their "only client."

> We are not puppets who unthinkingly parrot the position of big business or any other special interest group. We support our system of government, individual freedom, the free enterprise system, traditional concepts of private property rights and the reasonable use of one's property.
>
> Thus, in many of our cases our views have coincided with the views of the business community. That no more makes us a tool than did the protection of the Nazi party's constitutional rights make the American Civil Liberties Union a Nazi stooge.   [Momboisse, 1980b]

STRATEGIES

Sponsorship of cases has been the trademark both of the first and second wave of liberal interest group litigators, who attempted to bring cases to court in well-planned sequences. A major criticism of the conservative public interest law movement has been its reliance on the amicus curiae strategy. Horowitz has claimed that "One . . . policy for which many conservative public interest law firms have been properly criticized has been their striking penchant for amicus participation . . . . A high ratio of amicus participation on the part of a conservative public interest law firm raises a fair presumption that the firm is engaging in pufferies intended for naive audiences of donors, and not truly doing meaningful work" (1980: 67–68).

Horowitz's characterization, however, only partially reflects the movement. A closer look reveals some differences between those affiliated and unaffiliated with the National Legal Center for the Public Interest in terms of their reliance on the amicus curiae strategy. Most NLCPI-affiliated firms, however independent of the center they might be, have relied almost exclusively on the amicus curiae strategy at least in part because of NLCPI leaders' belief in the utility of this tactic. Whether such a belief stems from monetary considerations or strategic ones is somewhat unclear. But Hueter has claimed that "amicus curiae briefs can be important" when they address issues that the main parties fail to mention. In the same breath, however, he claimed that there is a "general feeling . . . [that the firms] might bring more cases to court" (Hueter, 1982).

The trend toward more sponsorship and less amicus curiae participation is already evident in the participation of two unaffiliated firms, the Washington Legal Foundation and the Pacific Legal Foundation. After participating almost exclusively as an amicus curiae during its early years, for example, the PLF is now concentrating on sponsorship so that it can set the "record straight" at the trial court level. In general, it believes that sponsorship allows for "broad public impact," whereas amicus curiae participation increases "presence" and visibility, which are no longer PLF priorities (Momboisse, 1982). The PLF used the amicus curiae strategy during its formative years to gain attention from the courts and the public. After accomplishing that goal, it moved away from amicus curiae participation so that it could have greater control and impact on the outcome of the litigation.

In contrast, the Washington Legal Foundation, though sponsoring most of its litigation, continues to rely on the amicus curiae. And, like groups that participate solely as an amicus curiae, WLF uses its briefs to counterbalance liberal groups when it cannot sponsor a case directly. In other words, it uses amicus curiae participation for impact rather than for organizational propaganda.

Currently, there is some variation among groups within the conservative public interest law movement regarding litigation strategy. The comments of leaders of both affiliated and unaffiliated firms indicate, however, that there is a definite trend toward direct sponsorship. Regardless of individual groups' reliance on participation as a direct sponsor or as an amicus curiae, however, one clear-cut difference emerges between liberal and conservative public interest law firms: the latter have not attempted to bring a series of test cases. Their participation has been reactive to circumstances or to pressure from liberal groups. The failure of these conservative groups to bring planned litigation to court, in the classic sense, does not necessarily imply that they are unconcerned with building precedent. The WLF, for example, has recently agreed to handle a highly visible case, *McCarthy*, in part to obtain expanded rights for the "average" crime victim.

As is the case with several other conservative and liberal litigators, the conservative public interest law firms wish to move away from the amicus curiae strategy. Those who rely on direct sponsorship as the prominent mode of participation, however, take a much different approach than their liberal counterparts. Instead of initiating a series of test cases, several of the conservative public interest law firms now sponsor suits to draw attention to their overall goals.

RESOURCES

Money. Attaining adequate funding for litigation has been problematic for many of the conservative public interest law firms. Although several foundations and businesses, including Scaife and Coors, have channeled money into some of the firms, the conservative public interest law movement has been plagued by two major problems: not only has there been competition among groups for funding but there have been some eyebrows raised over the reliance of conservative public interest law firms on contributions from business interests.

The competition began after the National Legal Center created the regional centers. By 1978 there were at least eight firms competing for a limited amount of money. And although the NCLPI, at least theoretically, was designed to help affiliated firms to raise funds, according to most of the firms involved it actually competed with the centers it created.

This situation is not unique to conservative public interest law firms. As both O'Connor (1980) and Berger (1979) have indicated, a plethora of women's groups, all vying for limited funds, hampered litigation efforts on behalf of women. Both analysts concluded that competition among women's groups led them to rely on the amicus curiae strategy because they could not afford the costs of direct sponsorship. The large number of conservative firms competing for funding has thus far affected the conservative side similarly. While many of the NLCPI-affiliated firms have expressed the desire to sponsor more cases, financial limitations have forced them to continue to rely on amicus curiae briefs.

Continued reliance on the amicus curiae strategy has in turn led some to bring into question the reliance of conservative public interest law firms on their major source of money to date — business interests. Instead of playing an ideological role in litigation, Horowitz noted, many conservative public interest law firms merely "kiss ass of business contributors" by participating as amici in cases with economic ramifications (Horowitz, 1983). Some firms may consequently have put themselves in a Catch-22 situation; by filing amici to appease contributors, they are failing to convince business to contribute because that sort of participation may not be effective. The financial picture of all the conservative firms is not entirely bleak. Some, including the wLF and the PLF, have managed to increase their budgets each year. Although the wLF used the direct mail strategy and receives contributions from members, like the PLF, it is primarily supported by businesses and foundations. These firms may have succeeded in attracting funding because unlike the regionals, they have escaped the Catch 22; they are sponsoring more cases, rather than continuing to file amicus curiae, and so have attracted the attention of the business community. Whether the regionals will be as successful in their fund-raising endeavors may depend on their ability to follow a similar path.

Government Support. Like the founders of the National Lawyers' Committee, those who established the first conservative public interest law firms were well connected with government. Zumbrun and Momboisse worked for Governor Reagan, and Popeo served as a government attorney during the Nixon administration. While leaders like these left government to found or to work for conservative public interest law firms, others actually left the movement to join the Reagan administration. James Watt was the first president of the Mountain States Legal Foundation, and Rex E. Lee, now solicitor general of the United States, was also connected with the MSLF (Lee, 1982).

Although it would seem that these firms would enjoy unusually easy access to government officials, given the ideological bent of the current administration, that assumption is erroneous for two reasons. First, some members of the Reagan administration have reported that the conservative public interest law firms have not taken full advantage of these ties. One individual claims that the

conservative firms "can't have a more sympathetic guy than me
. . . [in the executive branch] but they don't call me. . . . [I] get more
calls from traditional public interest law firms than conservative
public interest law firms." This assertion has been corroborated both
by Solicitor General Lee and by many conservative public interest
law firms — in fact, the Mountain States Legal Foundation claims
to have severed all ties with its former president, James Watt (Mellor,
1982). Apparently, despite having friends in the federal government,
the firms have not attempted to use those ties.

A second reason conservative public interest law firms have been
unable to foster intimate ties with the executive branch may explain
why they have not attracted "sympathizers"; these groups often challenge governmental practices in court. While this was more evident
during the Carter years, it continues under the Reagan administration. Some observers have concluded that regardless of administration, conservative public interest law will be needed (Horowitz, 1980,
Momboisse, 1982; Popeo, 1983).

A third explanation for the firms' failure to align themselves with
the federal government may lie more with geography than with
ideology. Five of the eight conservative firms considered here, unlike their liberal counterparts, are located outside of the District
of Columbia and do not maintain offices there. Analysts have criticized the conservative movement for not emulating the strategy of
the liberal firms, who were able to make inroads into the federal
government by establishing their headquarters in the District of
Columbia.

Although the distribution of conservative public interest law firms
throughout the United States has hampered their forming ties with
the federal government, it has helped them develop relationships
with the states. Momboisse claimed that state agencies often call
upon the services of the Pacific Legal Foundation when they want
their position defended by someone other than the state attorney
general. Similarly, the Washington Legal Foundation has recently
agreed to represent twenty-three states in a death penalty case. Other
regional conservative public interest law firms regularly file amicus curiae briefs in support of the positions of the states within their
regional jurisdictions.

Unlike liberal firms, the conservative public interest law firms
have not always attempted to maintain close ties with the executive

branch of the federal government, but have instead built up a rapport with state governments. It is a tactic expressing, perhaps, their
ideology and locale.

Longevity. The conservative public interest law firms generally
have attempted to increase their presence in litigation before the
U.S. Supreme Court (see figure 5-1). Many of the firms are still quite
new; nonetheless, this increasing participation indicates that although the firms may not be interested in bringing test cases to the
courts, they are concerned with creating favorable precedent and
with attaining repeat-player status.

Increasing participation, at least as amici, might only represent
some firms' attempts to appease their members. Clearly, the ability
of many of these firms to continue to participate hinges upon their

Figure 5-1

Participation of Conservative Public Interest Law Firms in
U.S. Supreme Court Litigation, 1973-1981 Terms*

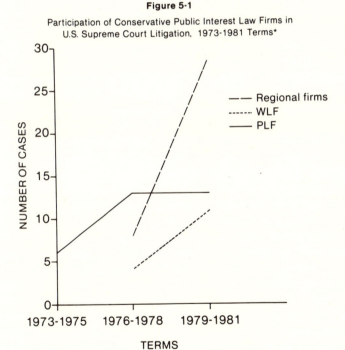

* Data Compiled by Author

attracting financial support. One of the best funded of these firms —
the PLF — has participated to date in more litigation than any of the
others. But the PLF is also the oldest of the modern-day firms. And
although younger firms seem to be participating more frequently,
it may be too early to predict their continued use of the courts, given
funding deficiencies they may face.

Staff. One of the major criticisms of the conservative public interest law movement has been its alleged inability to recruit expert
staff. Some analysts have asserted that unlike liberal firms, conservative firms have not attempted to recruit either outstanding law
school graduates or people committed to their cause (Horowitz, 1980;
Kristol, 1981). According to these commentators, the conservative
public interest law movement has not provided an ideological outlet for outstanding conservative graduates as liberal firms did for
liberal students in the late 1960s (see Broder, 1980). Such criticisms,
however, do not accurately describe the conservative public interest
law movement as a whole. Like strategies, the staff makeup of affiliated and unaffiliated firms differs.

One of Theberge's goals in creating the regional centers was to
attract leading conservatives into the leadership of the movement.
He was largely successful; many of the firms were and continue to
be led by prominent conservatives. Yet many of these individuals
were recruited from the ranks of business, and not from the legal
community. Christopher Bond, the first president of the Great Plains
Legal Foundation, was a president of the Chamber of Commerce
prior to his involvement with conservative public interest law. And
while he and several other of Theberge's original recruits brought
prestige to the movement, they failed to provide the legal expertise
so critical to the success of interest group litigation.

Criticizing the staffs of the unaffiliated firms for lack of expertise may be unjustified, however. The Washington Legal Foundation and the Pacific Legal Foundation were not only founded by
dedicated attorneys but have attempted by various means to supply fresh recruits for their ranks. They have attempted to attract
new staff members by establishing internship programs to train law
school students and graduates. Some of these interns have eventually joined their staffs. These firms have relied heavily on local institutions to provide them with promising law students. The WLF

relies on Georgetown University Law School, Popeo's alma mater, to supply it with recruits. Such recruitment of local students seems well suited to the ideology and purpose of these centers. Like their relationship with the states, rather than the federal government, the firms seem more content to work on conservative public interest law at a regional level, and therefore recruit staff from the local area.

A second means some conservative public interest law firms have used to attract good staff is to offer good salaries. Conservative public interest law firms will not reveal the starting salaries of their staff attorneys, but the pay of upper-echelon attorneys illustrates the difference between liberal and conservative firms. In 1980 Momboisse earned $65,000, for example, compared with $48,000 paid to the highest-paid liberal public interest law attorney, Sid Wolinsky of Public Advocates (Wood, 1981). The PLF and other firms hope that high salaries will help them to attract even the best local graduates.

There appears to be a substantial difference between the staffs of the affiliated and the unaffiliated firms. Starting out with politically conservative, well-known businessmen and women, the staffs of some of the unaffiliated centers have stagnated. The unaffiliated centers, however, not only started with capable bases of experienced attorneys, but have attempted to attract new legal talent.

Publicity. Of all the resources considered important to litigation efforts, publicity is the one receiving the greatest use by the conservative firms. They vary the type of publicity they employ, but most have recognized its importance.

Most commonly used among conservative firms is the monograph. The National Legal Center and the Washington Legal Foundation issue studies conducted by well-known individuals on a variety of areas of interest. The following note, which accompanied a WLF monograph (McDonald, 1982), explains the general purpose of these publications:

Dear Friend:
    Enclosed is a copy of a legal public policy monograph published by the Washington Legal Foundation (WLF) in order to provide the national legal community with much-needed legal studies on a variety of timely public policy issues.

With 200,000 members and supporters, WLF is America's largest public interest law center. The enclosed is one of a series of legal/academic policy studies commissioned by WLF which focus upon matters affecting the judiciary, the judicial process, the criminal justice system and free enterprise.

These publications are provided as a service primarily to Federal and State judges, law school professors and their students, business leaders, the media, legislators and the interested public to aid in public debate and deliberations on critical matters affecting the public interest.

We invite your comments on the value of this monograph and would be most receptive to your suggestions regarding other important issues worthy of scholarly treatment in future legal public policy studies by the Washington Legal Foundation and its Texas Division.

Sincerely,

Daniel J. Popeo
General Counsel

The WLF and several others, such as the Equal Employment Advisory Council, use these pamphlets to disseminate their views on particular policy matters.

Somewhat surprisingly, the monographs themselves have been the subject of some controversy within the conservative community. On one hand, some suggest that the National Legal Center especially should be doing more of this sort of activity. According to one individual, NLCPI attorneys "are fools because they don't grab that educational role." Others, on the other hand, suggest that the conservative firms should not divert scarce resources to the publication of monographs, because they cannot simultaneously be "publishing houses, educational groups, and litigating centers."

There does appear to be some consensus on the utility of the more traditional lobbying avenue: the law review. Pacific Legal Foundation attorneys have recently begun to write articles for law reviews, including the *Family Law Quarterly*, *Pacific Law Journal*, *Pepperdine Law Journal*, and the American Bar Association's *Urban Lawyer*, among others (PLF, 1979–80:12). In addition, Popeo has attempted to develop ties with law school professors who may help the WLF's litigation efforts by writing favorable law review articles. More recently, NLCPI attorney William Howard has started to work on the creation of the *New Federalist*, a law journal tentatively planned to be headquartered at Harvard Law School. Through this journal, the NLCPI hopes to cultivate young legal talent and to create a more receptive judicial environment by putting together a prestigious editorial board that will command the attention of the entire judicial community.

While conservatives have applauded the National Legal Center's efforts, some say that the "NLCPI is not vital enough to recognize the value of that [law journal] project." Whether or not this criticism is justified, the law review project may provide conservative public interest law firms with a viable publicity outlet, regardless of the NLCPI's involvement or noninvolvement.

While many of the conservative public interest law firms have sought publicity through monographs and law reviews, the Washington Legal Foundation has employed a unique method. In 1981, it established a Court Watch Project to "promote public scrutiny and accountability of prosecutors, judges and parole boards who are too lenient with criminals at the expense of crime victims and the law-abiding public" (WLF, 1982b:4). To achieve this objective the WLF developed a victims' impact statement, which it uses to assess officials' "insensitivity" to victims of crime. After examining these statements, which are filled out by WLF supporters, the organization has launched investigations into the court decisions of more than one hundred local, state, and federal judges (WLF, 1982b; Marcus, 1982).

Although this program clearly "fits" the Washington Legal Foundation's goal of expanding the rights of victims of crimes, it is unclear what effect its reports will have on the judiciary. Whether WLF activities, which resemble those of other groups that believe judges have been too lax, will be totally ineffective, create an inhospitable judiciary, or intimidate judges to act in accordance with its philosophy are important questions.

Conservative firms have recognized the importance of publicity, but the means they have used thus far have apparently had little impact. One exception may be the more traditional use of law reviews. But as these programs are in their developmental stages still, it is difficult to assess what effect, if any, they will have on the judicial climate in the United States.

Intergroup Support.   As initially planned by Theberge, the regional centers were to work together as one cohesive network. The National Legal Center was supposed to play a major role in fostering cooperation so that "the right hand knew what the left hand was doing" (Hueter, 1982). There has been some cooperation among firms, but it has not been of the kind Theberge envisioned. The NLCPI not only failed to play the role of coordinator, but actually competed with its member firms for limited resources. The Pacific Legal Foundation, which opposed its creation, initially felt "animosity and distrust" for the NLCPI. Although competition among firms has not been eliminated, there is some evidence that it has begun to fade. Most of the firms send representatives to the Heritage Foundation luncheons, where they can communicate about cases of interest and mutual problems. Many of the firms believe that it is important to keep abreast of each other's litigation activities to avoid needless duplication in litigation. In sum, though there has been some hostility and competition among firms, they apparently intend to continue the "non-cooperation" strategy, which seems to characterize the litigation efforts of the range of conservative litigators.

SUCCESS

Studies of liberal public interest law firms note changes in the law and a universal acceptance of the liberal definition of the public interest as indicators of their success. Because the conservative public interest law firms were founded to change or to reverse these two trends, their ability to do so provides at least one way to judge the success of conservative public interest law in the United States.

Any discussion of the ability of the conservative public interest law movement to bring about such changes, however, must be couched in terms of the unease that conservatives generally have about litigation tactics and the use of the courts to advance their ideas. Changes in the law and/or in the universal acceptance of the liberal definition of the public interest has created some division within conservative ranks. Unlike liberals, conservatives are divided over the very use of the courts. Many are reluctant to advocate judicial activism, regardless of ideological bent. According to one conservative:

> I think they [conservative public interest law firms] have been tactically wise and strategically unwise. Tactically wise because by cluttering up the courts with ideological pursuits, they have at least made clear

> to some neutrals left in this country that conservatives can screw up
> the legal system as well as liberals — making it possible, in the long run,
> for a consensus to develop again in the country which is hostile to the
> overuse of the legal process. [Silberman, 1981:18]

In short, conservative firms have not received the support of the
entire conservative community.

It is not surprising that, unlike their liberal counterparts, conservative firms so far have neither changed the law nor to any significant extent developed new areas of the law. In most instances,
conservatives have not tried to do this; rather, they have attempted
to provide a counterbalance to liberal groups in areas of the law
that liberals created — environmental and consumer protection, for
example. To this end, conservative public interest law firms have
made some headway. For example, during the 1981 term of the
United States Supreme Court, in 33 percent of the cases in which
a liberal group participated, at least one conservative firm was present to counterbalance liberal claims when another conservative
group was not already representing that position.

The conservative public interest law firms themselves believe
that they are significantly affecting the activities of liberal groups.
"wlf fills a unique and vital role in the national legal public policy
arena," says Popeo. "wlf has consistently proven itself to be the
only effective alternative in the courts to the anti-business, pro-
criminal groups like the aclu, the naacp ldf, Public Citizen Litigation Group and other Ralph Nader organizations" (wlf, 1982a:4).
Similarly, the Pacific Legal Foundation has claimed: "When the plf
first began speaking for mainstream America, special interest groups
cried foul. But plf kept speaking. Foundation attorneys went where
they were not welcome. They challenged the record. . . . Greater
balance was brought to the courtroom and to the market place of
ideas" (plf, 1981–82:1).

Presenting a counterbalance to liberal interests in court is, of
course, intimately connected with the opposition to what some have
called liberal public interest law firms' second success: "a moral
monopoly on the definition of the public interest." Many conservative leaders, recognizing that they have not eradicated the liberal
version of the public interest, have nevertheless claimed that their
firms at least have succeeded in introducing their views in court.

Popeo has characterized the courts now as "battleground[s] for the supremacy of ideas in this country" (Popeo, 1981).

Liberal groups have been quick to criticize conservative firms, calling their definition of the public interest merely an inflated version of the business perspective.[7] Sid Wolinsky of Public Advocates said:

> I think calling it [the PLF] a public interest law firm is a perversion of the English language. It should be called a corporate enterprise law firm. A public interest law firm represents groups of the public that are underrepresented, such as minority groups.
>
> PLF doesn't fit that at all. Under the rubric of public interest, it really is a heavily funded, well-financed corporate interest law firm.   [quoted in Wood, 1981]

Nader has leveled similar charges at the conservative public interest law movement. "My idea of a public interest lawyer is someone who isn't funded by special interests and who is guided by their conscience. Not these guys. They're in it for the money. I think they get good contracts. Just watch, now they're hob-nobbing with the heads of companies and pretty soon . . . they'll be general counsels of corporations" (quoted in Schmitt, 1979). Whether or not these and similar charges are justified is unimportant at this point. What is clear, as the preceding quotes reveal, is that liberal organizations have been forced to take notice of the growth of the conservative public interest law movement in the United States.

But whether or not "the public interest legal movement which favors less government can effectively redefine the meaning of public interest law in the 1980s" (Popeo, 1981) is questionable at this point. Unlike the liberal movement, the conservative firms have not attained the full support of the conservative community. Moreover, there continues to be some competition among groups, resulting in a splintered, rather than cohesive, movement. Even if these and other similar problems can be overcome, conservatives face an uphill struggle. The eradication of a well-entrenched view of the public interest will continue to provide a difficult challenge for conservative firms.

 # AN ASSESSMENT OF THE STATUS OF INTEREST GROUP LITIGATION

The assumptions political scientists have made about the litigation of all interest groups have been examined for their applicability to conservative groups involved in economic, social, and public interest litigation. However, their appropriateness for describing the litigation of conservative groups collectively has not been probed. In this chapter, each assumption will be explored in the expectation that knowing more about their "fit" in the case of conservative groups will increase our understanding of interest group litigation generally.

Resort to the Courts

It has been widely assumed that only politically disadvantaged groups resort to litigation. This assumption indeed describes accurately the behavior both of liberal groups and of early conservative interest groups. Organizations such as the Maryland League for State Defense and the American Constitutional League went to court when they failed to accomplish their goals in other political spheres. As time went on, however, and more liberal groups became involved in litigation, conservative organizations, including many with political clout, came to view themselves as disadvantaged in the *judicial* arena. Many conservatives, aware that liberals were achieving their goals in court, recognized the need to enter the judicial forum to use the courts to their own advantage and to counteract the liberal groups' success. Besides recognizing their judicial disadvantage, they recognized the growing role of the courts, particularly the Supreme Court, in society. The courts in conservative eyes have become "policy makers" that were closely allied with liberal interests.

The idea that only politically disadvantaged groups resort to litigation is actually timebound. Because scholars repeatedly examined similar groups that took to the courts during the same eras, they repeatedly reached the same explanation for group resort to litigation. This new look at the conservative groups reveals that the traditional explanation is applicable only to the early conservative groups and must be modified to explain the motives of today's litigators. They view themselves as disadvantaged only in the judicial forum and thus have resorted to the courts more offensively than defensively.

The finding that "advantaged" as well as "disadvantaged" groups resort to the courts has important implications for future study of interest group litigation. Rather than assuming that only groups lacking in political clout will take up litigation, we can now propose that a wide range of groups regularly resort to the judicial arena because they view the courts as just another political battlefield, which they must enter to fight for their goals. Courtrooms, in fact, may no longer be much different from legislative corridors, which often serve as arenas for competing group interests.

STRATEGIES

Scholars have long said that interest group litigators prefer the sponsorship to amicus curiae strategy. This indeed seems to be true of the early conservative litigators, who filed amicus curiae briefs only if their position was already being handled by an ally. Most latter-day conservative groups also prefer sponsorship. Even most of those who were not employing that tactic at the time my study was conducted said they intended to sponsor more cases in the future. The single most important reason they gave for preferring this strategy resembled what scholars have long suggested: sponsorship allows a group to control the course of litigation, especially if the case is handled from the trial court level.

But even this assumption must be modified if it is to reflect accurately the activities of all the groups. The socially conservative litigators have a unique problem. Unlike liberal groups involved in social litigation, which often litigate against governmental restrictions, the conservatives are generally on the same side as government. In order to sponsor litigation, these groups must obtain government permission. Although at times they have opted for this National Consumers' League type of strategy, the AUL Legal Defense Fund and Citizens for Decency through Law also have attempted to intervene in litigation. These groups often found that state and federal attorneys were unwilling or unable to defend their position, yet they wanted to be a party to the suit and not just a "friend."

Two of the groups, however, the Equal Employment Advisory Council and Americans for Effective Law Enforcement, can be categorized as amicus curiae organizations. Each participates solely as an amicus in litigation and neither has any plans to alter that preference. AELE and EEAC are motivated by different forces, but they have given similar reasons for their reliance on the amicus strategy. Both feel that they can concentrate only on issues of interest to them. The groups argue that the amicus curiae, when used this way, can just as effectively whittle away or build precedent as direct sponsorship can.

The traditional understanding of group strategies in court, though still generally valid, must be modified to take into account the new breed of amicus curiae litigator. Yet future studies of interest group use of the courts can safely operate under the assumption that regardless of the specific strategy used, all groups have one goal — to build favorable precedent. One case may be important, but it is the long-term effect of litigation with which most groups are concerned. The fact that precedent building is the essence of interest group litigation should not be surprising if we consider the differences between the courts and the legislatures. Even though both may now be characterized by the presence of competing interests, those arenas differ in the nature of their decision making. The strategies used by groups in the judicial arena, whether sponsorship or amicus curiae, show that groups are well aware of these differences and in fact have molded their tactics to conform with the norms of the judicial forum.

RESOURCES

Previous studies have suggested that the six factors outlined below are used by all interest groups to maximize their litigation efforts. This book concurs, but with some demurrers and modifications.

Money. Adequate funding is universally significant: all groups, regardless of ideological bent, motivating force, or issue concern, need money to litigate. And as Karen O'Connor has suggested, the requisite amount of funding seems to vary with strategic choice. Groups using or expecting to use the direct sponsorship strategy need more funds than those solely filing amicus curiae briefs. And this is evident in the intensity of their fund-raising efforts.

Beyond this similarity between different ideological groups, several other interesting findings emerge from this study concerning financial resources. Most of the conservative groups examined have a common tie: direct mail fund raiser Richard Viguerie. During the early 1970s most of the groups retained Viguerie, who succeeded in raising substantial funds for them. Yet the overhead costs of his operation, among other factors, have led them to forgo using his services. A second and perhaps more profitable common tie among the organizations is the Scaife Family Foundation. Like the Ford Foundation's relationship with liberal groups, which includes both financial support and advice, Scaife's relationship with conservative groups has provided some of the organizations with substantial funds and guidance.

Because money is so critical, the conservative groups may soon be in better financial shape than some of their liberal counterparts. As Scaife and others continue to channel funds into conservative groups, Ford has continued to cut back on its funding of liberal groups (see Clark, 1980; Singer, 1979; Terris, 1974). Although financial concerns hampered several of the groups' ability to litigate early on, some are now obtaining funding from sources similar to those used by liberal groups. Even with foundation funding, however, it may be some time before all the conservative groups "catch up" financially with their older liberal counterparts.

In short, the necessity of adequate funding (and for many groups the lack thereof), will lead to continued use of the amicus curiae strategy. Only those groups, both liberal and conservative, that can raise substantial funds will be able to sponsor cases, the preferred strategy of most litigators.

Government Support. Like funding, support from the Solicitor General's Office, generally in the form of compatible amicus curiae briefs, is often mentioned as a critical resource. But not all conservative group litigators enjoy the same relationship with the solicitor general or with governments. The exact relationship seems to depend on the type of group.

The conservatives involved in social litigation most resemble the liberal groups; they view governments as desirable allies because of the type of issues they litigate. Unlike the liberal groups, however, which often attempt to co-opt the support of the U.S. government in cases involving private claims of discrimination, the social conservatives have supported the states and the federal government through compatible amicus curiae briefs.

But even this congenial relationship has varied, depending on the administration in office. The Americans United for Life Legal Defense Fund found the government much more supportive of its objectives during the Nixon years than during the Carter administration. In fact, this is why it intervened in the 1980 funding cases. But except for some variation due to the ideology of the administration, the socially conservative groups have enjoyed generally congenial relations with the state and federal governments.

In contrast, the economic groups have not been particularly friendly with either the states or the federal government. They generally view the government as "the" opposition in litigation, regardless of administration because of the issues in question. Many of these groups see themselves as monitors of excessive government regulation.

The relationship between the conservative public interest law firms and government is perhaps the most interesting of all. Although the conservative public interest law firms have not attempted to cooperate with the federal government, they have fostered intimate ties with the states, a consequence perhaps not only of their geographic locations, but also of the cause that motivates them. On economic issues, these groups resemble the economic conservatives; they view the public interest as best represented when government stays out of the private sphere. Consequently, cooperation between

the conservative public interest law firms and the federal government is unlikely, regardless of administration. On social issues, however, the conservative public interest law firms share views with the
social litigators. It is therefore not surprising that, like the social
groups, the conservative public interest law firms have aligned themselves with the states on these issues.

It appears that the importance of government support as a resource became ingrained in the literature because scholarly interest focused exclusively on certain types of groups. When the range
of groups is examined and the relationships with governments of
all levels are scrutinized, the pattern appears to be far more varied
and substantially affected by the kinds of issues at stake. Future work
in this area should not operate under the assumption that federal
government support is necessarily critical for all groups. The need,
and even the desire, for such assistance depends on the issues at stake.

Longevity.   In this study longevity has been defined as the increasing use of the courts over time. Scholars' belief in the utility of groups'
use of this resource is universal. Indeed, most of the conservatives,
like their liberal counterparts, have increased their litigation activities. As indicated in figure 6-1, by the 1980 term of the Supreme
Court conservative groups appeared in over 50 percent of the cases
in which an interest group was present, whether as amicus curiae,
direct sponsor, or intervenor (O'Connor and Epstein, 1983a).

All the conservative groups are well on their way to achieving,
if they have not already achieved, repeat-player status. Nonetheless, their ability to mount further litigation may hinge on finances.

Though longevity appears to be an equally important resource
for liberal and conservative groups, it may be too soon to assess
whether this will continue to be the case. Like the decision to pursue (or not to pursue) various strategies, a group's increasing use
of the courts may hinge upon its ability to obtain adequate funding. Nonetheless, it is clear that all interest groups view increasing
use of the courts as an important way to increase their success in
the judicial arena.

Staff.   Whatever tactics an interest group may select, the quality
of its staff is a critical resource. There is one significant difference
between the ways liberal and conservative groups have maintained

Figure 6-1

Participation of Conservative and Liberal Groups in
U.S. Supreme Court Litigation, 1969-1980 Terms*

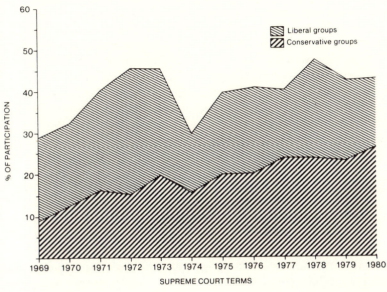

* Source: O'Connor and Epstein, 1983b:481

and cultivated staff expertise: conservatives apparently view stability of the staff as more important than the regular injection of new blood into the organization, while the liberals seem to think a steady supply of newcomers is more important than staff stability.

Several conservative groups have developed internship programs, but the staffs of these groups have nonetheless remained unchanged over the past several years. Moreover, they have been associated with one or two "important" individuals. The advantages of this sort of staff policy are clear; there is continuity to a group's litigation efforts and there are clearly established goals for the organization.

Yet, as some liberal groups have found, there are also advantages to bringing in new staffers. New attorneys can bring creative, innovative ideas to the organization. One observer of public interest law asks: "How have [the 'Naderites'] succeeded so well? Are they brilliant lawyers? No, they are no more brilliant than conservative lawyers. They just didn't know what you couldn't do in court, and they went into court and, after being rebuffed quite a few times, they discovered they could do it" (Kristol, 1981:27). In addition, reliance on one individual within an organization can cause problems. If that individual leaves, the group's very survival may be put into question.

Recognizing these problems, but also keeping in mind the advantages of maintaining stability in staff, several conservative organizations have tried to bring in new attorneys. The organizations that have attempted to maintain the delicate balance between stability and change have been successful, although in some instances their success or failure may still have to be proven. In any event, it is clear that conservatives and liberals have cultivated expertise differently. On the whole, conservative staffs are characterized more by stability than by change.

This difference provides an interesting issue for future research. The advantages of stability over change should be examined in greater detail as the conservative groups increase their presence in the judicial arena.

Publicity.   Like their liberal counterparts, almost all the conservative groups have recognized the importance of both traditional and nontraditional means of creating a favorable judicial climate. Liberal groups have relied on the law review; conservative groups have used more flamboyant lobbying devices.

Endorsing others' publications or publishing their own books and monograph series are strategies few liberal groups have used. Even though there is some disagreement within the conservative community over the utility of these devices, the groups are proud of their ability to produce such materials. With the exception of one of the Equal Employment Advisory Council's publications, however, these books and monographs have yet to be cited by the U.S. Supreme Court. Whether or not conservative groups begin to get more concrete results like Supreme Court citation for their work in this area may determine the fate of this tactic. If it proves to be useful, liberal groups might even decide to make use of such techniques.

Intergroup Support. One of the most common traits of conservative groups has been their tendency to refrain from cooperation in litigation. Liberal groups often file amicus curiae briefs in support of each other's efforts, but the conservative groups have avoided what they consider "me-too" participation, with the intention of eliminating needless duplication of effort.

Noncooperation in litigation does not, however, imply lack of coordination outside the courtroom. Indeed, to pursue a strategy of noncooperation, groups must know in advance which groups will be participating in what cases. To facilitate the exchange of the necessary information, the Heritage Foundation holds monthly luncheons, which most of the groups studied in these pages attend. Also, groups with like-minded interests such as the Equal Employment Advisory Council and the National Chamber Litigation Center often communicate by telephone. In short, unlike their liberal counterparts, conservatives have avoided cooperation in litigation by establishing a coordinated network to facilitate the planning of that strategy.

This difference provides another interesting issue for future research. For years scholars have operated under the assumption that cooperation, generally through the filing of compatible amicus briefs, has helped interest groups in court. Now that funds for liberal groups appear to be diminishing, such in-court cooperation may become rarer among these groups, too. If liberals choose to organize out-of-court networks and whether this will affect their litigation are two questions that future work may wish to address in light of the findings presented here.

SUCCESS AND FUTURE OF
CONSERVATIVE INTEREST GROUP LITIGATION

The groups studied here are relatively new. Only three — Citizens for Decency through Law, Americans for Effective Law Enforcement, and the National Right to Work Legal Defense Foundation — were created before 1970. In contrast, when Clement Vose studied the NAACP Legal Defense Fund's efforts, the NAACP was almost fifty years old and the Legal Defense Fund almost twenty. The difference in maturity of the liberal and conservative organizations is most evident when one compares their success rates. Regardless of the measure used, it is more difficult to assess the success of the newer conservative groups; the conservative public interest law firms, in particular, are just beginning to "get their feet wet." Older groups are more successful in litigation — each has made a name for itself, each has become more proficient in litigation, and each has profited from the increasing conservatism of the Burger Court.

The ability of the newer groups to attain their objectives in court hinges on similar factors, to say nothing of their need for sufficient funding. Many of the newer groups, including the National Chamber Litigation Center and the conservative public interest law firms, wish to sponsor more cases and to otherwise increase their litigation activities. Doing so would increase their proficiency in litigation and allow them to attain repeat-player status, but their ability to achieve such goals depends upon their ability to attract adequate funding.

Assuming that such resources will be available, conservative interest group litigation will become an increasingly important phenomenon deserving of further study. Clearly, it will more than ever before put the Court in the position of having to mediate between competing group interests. Judicial politics, in fact, may not be significantly different from the legislative and executive processes, which are widely understood to be characterized by the presence of competing group interests.

NOTES

Chapter One

1. Until the 1960s, the NAACP and its Legal Defense Fund operated virtually as one. When Thurgood Marshall, the Legal Defense Fund's general counsel, was replaced in 1961 by Jack Greenberg, tensions between the two organizations mounted, ultimately resulting in a complete split. The hostility between the two organizations reached its apex in 1983, when the NAACP successfully sued the NAACP Legal Defense Fund to prevent it from using the NAACP name.

2. In 1906 National Consumers' League members realized that state attorneys general would be unreliable when a New York ruling concerning the state maximum hour law was appealed. Although an assistant New York attorney general argued and won the case in the Supreme Court of New York, he did not show up to represent the state in appellate court (see Goldmark, 1953).

3. Louis Brandeis was associated with the National Consumers' League from 1907 to 1915. After Brandeis was nominated to serve on the U.S. Supreme Court, Felix Frankfurter, another future Supreme Court justice, agreed to litigate for the National Consumers' League. Thurgood Marshall served on the staff of the NAACP from 1934 to 1961 and was instrumental in the creation of the Legal Defense Fund in 1939.

4. Derived from Vose, 1982; see also the References section in this book.

5. Other areas of interest include environmental issues (Anderson, 1973; Cook, 1980; Liroff, 1977; Rosenbaum, 1973; Trubek, 1978) and free speech cases (Berns, 1957; Cortner, 1975, 1980; Dorsen, 1968; Halpern, 1976; Johnson, 1963; Markmann, 1965; Neier, 1979; Rabin, 1976; Reitman, 1975; Westin, 1962).

6. Amicus curiae briefs can be filed prior to the Court's consideration of a jurisdictional statement or a petition for certiorari. The Court's rules, however, state that "such motions are not favored" (338 U.S. at 959–60).

7. The justices of the Court apparently recognized this, and in 1949 changed their rules to make amicus curiae participation more difficult (see O'Connor and Epstein, 1983c).

Chapter Two

1. When the union could not afford to pay this sum, the AFL issued a call "to the entire labor movement, urging the workers to contribute an hour's pay . . . toward the payment of the judgment. The day on which the hour's work was to be contributed was designated as the Hatters Day" (Lieberman, 1950:66). These funds were eventually collected and Loewe was paid.

2. This discussion is drawn largely from Wood (1968).

3. Johnson, for example, had been offered a position on the U.S. Supreme Court by two presidents, James Garfield and Grover Cleveland (see Twiss, 1942:208).

4. Twiss was puzzled by how Dagenhart brought this case to the courts. "Just how Mr. Dagenhart could afford leading New York lawyers when he was dependent upon his child's labor . . . is another question whose answer would shed light on how our constitutional law is made" (Twiss, 1942:228-29).

5. The committee also sponsored *Bailey v. Drexel Furniture* (1922); see Wood, 1968.

6. The NELA, which was established in 1885, ran into major difficulties because of its "unwieldy and heterogeneous" membership (see *Business Week*, 25 January 1933:12) and because of the poor reputation it developed through its use of propaganda. According to several sources, NELA's "political and propaganda activities" were so widely criticized that the Federal Trade Commission eventually launched an investigation of the organization (*New York Times*, 13 January 1933:1; *Business Week*, 25 January 1933:12).

7. The initial idea for a law that would address the high infant and maternity mortality rates in the United States was a direct outgrowth of the suffrage movement. Papachristou declares: "The struggle for the 19th Amendment had aroused women's interests and energy and utilized their talents and passions as never before. . . . The tendency to come together in groups and the reforming zeal of Progressivism seemed robust. . . . Many reform activities were taking place, as women investigated labor conditions, [and] tried to secure protective laws for female and child labor" (1976:187). But it took the efforts of the Women's Joint Congressional Committee to translate those ideas into solid proposals. Formed in 1920 as a women's lobbying group, the committee represented a coalition of the more important women's groups (see Papachristou, 1976:190 for a list of its constituent members). Two of its primary goals included passage of the Sheppard-Towner Maternity Act and of a child labor amendment.

8. It was no coincidence, then, that when Shouse announced the for-

mation of the Liberty League in August 1934, he claimed that it would be organized like the Association Against the Prohibition Amendment (see *New York Times*, 23 August 1934:1). The members of the old AAPA realized that "the Liberty League could lay claim to a rich heritage of practical experience and the successful application of conservative ideas" (Keller, 1958:257), as was done during repeal.

9. Interestingly, both the majority and dissenting opinions in *NAACP v. Button* (1963) referred to the ABA Committee's opinion.

10. Between 1935 and 1936 the National Lawyers' Committee issued reports on the following laws: National Labor Relations Act, Bituminous Coal Act, Potato Act, Agricultural Adjustment Act, and Social Security.

11. A similar strategy was used by the National Lawyers' Committee in challenging the Guffey Bituminous Coal Act, which created certain codes for the mining industry. Three months after Reed's subcommittee attacked the National Labor Relations Act, J. Van Dyke Norman's subcommittee on the Coal Act issued a report similarly challenging the act's legality. Norman later "withdrew" as chair because he represented Carter Coal Company's successful challenge of the act (Twiss, 1942:247; Cortner, 1964:100).

Chapter Three

1. There is disagreement about the genesis of the right-to-work movement of the 1940s. Lieberman asserts that "immediately after the Wagner Act was declared constitutional" several Texas businessmen formed the Christian American Association, whose motto, the "American Way," was often supported by such slogans as "right-to-work" (Lieberman, 1950:332–33). But Pollitt claims that as early as 1936 "there was something called the 'right-to-work union' but little is known of its activities" (Pollitt, 1973:21).

2. The National Right to Work Committee attorneys petitioned the Court to argue orally, but their application was denied (350 U.S. 391).

3. Another area of major concern to the National Right to Work Legal Defense Foundation is union violence. In 1982, a foundation attorney signed a movie contract for the story of a union violence case, which will be promoted as the answer to *Norma Rae* (Cameron, 1982).

4. According to the National Right to Work Legal Defense Foundation, the only adverse precedent established before its creation was *International Association of Machinists v. Street* (1961). In that case, the U.S. Supreme Court claimed that union abuse of compulsory funds was illegal, but it gave workers few legal remedies to end such activity.

5. While the 1970 Court of Appeals decision in *Seay* provided the National Right to Work Legal Defense Foundation with an important precedent, the case was not fully settled until 1977. Three years after the court of appeals' decision, a district court dismissed the suit because the union created a refund procedure. But because of subsequent foundation victo-

ries and other decisions, in 1977 the union paid, in full, the compulsory fees back to the employees.

6. In defense of their position, National Right to Work leaders were forced to spend long hours giving testimony and providing depositions. This testimony revealed that 84 percent of the committee's and 44 percent of the foundation's funds came from employers (Sklar, 1979). But the names of those contributors have yet to be disclosed in open court.

7. In a Georgia-based union violence case, National Right to Work Legal Defense Foundation staff attorney Bruce Cameron maintained contact with the Atlanta-based Southeastern Legal Foundation because he and the attorney at the Southeastern Foundation had attended Emory University Law School together (Cameron, 1982).

8. It should be noted that the Federal Election Commission (FEC) suit was filed shortly after the National Right to Work Committee had filed a complaint with the FEC charging the AFL-CIO with "massive violations" of FECA.

9. Some claim that another repercussion of the union suit has been a change in attitude on the part of National Right to Work leaders. This change was well illustrated in 1977, when two long-time members of the committee's public relations staff quit, claiming that the committee and Larson had abandoned "that careful stance [against compulsory unionism] for a flat anti-union posture" (see *Wall Street Journal*, 13 September 1977:1; *U.S. News*, 1979:93–94).

10. Various organizations have provided different estimates for the cost of filing an amicus curiae. One National Chamber Litigation Center attorney, for example, indicated that briefs can cost as much as $20,000 (Wermeil, 1982:2), while an EEAC attorney estimated a range of $6,000 to $12,000.

11. The EEAC is actually considered a client of that labor law firm.

Chapter Four

1. Citizens for Decency through Law attorneys also motioned the Court to argue orally as an amicus curiae. The Court, however, rejected this motion (382 U.S. 934).

2. Citizens for Decency through Law was unsuccessful during this period, but in *Miller v. California* (1973) the United States Supreme Court promulgated a definition of obscenity that better served CDL's purposes than that set forth in *Roth*. CDL, however, did not participate in the *Miller* litigation.

3. Although Viguerie raised $2.3 million for Citizens for Decency through Law, according to one source between 81 and 84 percent of those funds "went back" to him (Crawford, 1980:62).

4. Several other groups participate in litigation on behalf of anti-abortion forces. The National Right to Life Committee, for example, was

involved in the 1982 term abortion litigation. Additionally, the Pro-Life Legal Defense Fund of Boston has participated in several Massachusetts cases, including *Bellotti v. Baird* (1979). But because of the AUL fund's status as the only full-time interest group litigator for the anti-abortion movement, many groups consider it "the" anti-abortion forces' representative in court nationwide.

5. In 1981 Henry Hyde joined the Board of Directors of Americans United for Life.

Chapter Five

1. Momboisse has claimed that "the pattern now is to get away from" amicus curiae participation so that the organization can keep tighter reins on the course of the litigation (Momboisse, 1982).

2. In 1981 the Great Plains and the Gulf Coast Legal Foundations merged because of problems they were encountering while attempting to operate individually. In 1982 they were joined by another fledgling center, the Legal Foundation of America.

3. Horowitz claimed that the National Legal Center would have to institute three changes before it could be a vital organization. First, it must break off relations with any one conservative public interest law firm or set of firms. Second, it should employ capable evaluators to suggest policy changes. Third, it should relent its alleged "coordinative" role. (1980: 51–52).

4. At the time of this writing (1984), other independent firms include the New England Legal Foundation, the Urban Legal Foundation, the American Legal Foundation, the Conservative Legal Defense Fund, and the U.S. Justice Foundation. Another firm, the Legal Foundation of America, recently affiliated itself with the Great Plains–Gulf Coast Legal Foundation.

5. Popeo, however, likes to refer to Nader as the Dan Popeo of the left (see McCaughey, 1980).

6. Popeo claimed that when he first established the WLF as an unaffiliated center, he received some "nasty" letters, stating that he was going to duplicate "what everyone else was doing." But since then some of the hostility has dissipated (Popeo, 1983).

7. There has, of course, been some name calling on both sides. Popeo often refers to the ACLU as the "American Criminal Lovers Union" and to the NAACP LDF as "professional racists" (see Rees, 1982; Whitney, 1982).

 # LIST OF INTEREST GROUPS

American Anti-Boycott Association. The association, later renamed the League for Industrial Rights, was formed in 1902 by manufacturers who were concerned about the potential effectiveness of unions' boycott activities. The association placed great emphasis on litigation to combat organized laborers' actions.

American Bar Association (ABA). The ABA was established in 1878 to serve as a voluntary national association for attorneys. Since its inception, the ABA has established a number of committees so that it can have an impact on public policy. Its Committee on the Judiciary, for example, rates the professional qualifications of nominees for federal judgeships.

American Civil Liberties Union (ACLU). The ACLU was founded in 1920 to defend union workers and draft evaders. Since that time, its activities have expanded into numerous areas of civil liberties and rights, including church-state relations and the death penalty.

ACLU Reproductive Freedom Project (RFP). The RFP was established in 1974 by the ACLU. It was specifically created to help coordinate pro-choice abortion rights litigation. Since its founding, it has been involved in several major abortion cases.

ACLU Women's Rights Project (WRP). The WRP is a special project of the ACLU that was established in 1971 specifically to litigate on behalf of women's rights. It has played a major role in most land-mark sex discrimination cases since.

American Constitutional League (ACL). The ACL was organized in late 1917. It was envisioned as a states' rights advocate by its creator, Everett Wheeler, the founder of the older Man Suffrage Association Opposed to Political Suffrage for Women.

American Federation of Labor-Congress of Industrial Organizations (AFL-CIO). The AFL-CIO was formed by a merger of the American Federation of Labor and Congress of Industrial Organizations in 1955 as a federation of national, state, city, and local unions. Currently located in Washington, D.C., it is the umbrella organization for more than one hundred unions. It lobbies and litigates in a broad range of issues affecting workers, including wages, working conditions, and immigration. Its political action committee, formed in 1956, was one of the first of its kind.

American Liberty League. The league was founded as an anti-New Deal group by many who had had close ties to the earlier movement to repeal the prohibition amendment. It was heavily funded by the du Ponts when it was established in 1934. Some viewed it as an effort to unseat Roosevelt in the next election.

American Public Health Association (APHA). The APHA was formed in 1872 to promote "personal and environmental health." It has filed amicus curiae briefs in several abortion cases, including *Roe v. Wade* (1973), in which the Supreme Court's majority opinion cited the APHA's brief.

Americans for Effective Law Enforcement (AELE). Formed in 1968 by Professor Fred Inbau, AELE was specifically created to reverse the Warren Court's liberal decisions in the area of criminal rights and to counteract the arguments of liberal groups in this area. Because it believes that prosecutors well represent its interests in court, the AELE participates solely as an amicus curiae.

Americans United for Life (AUL). AUL was established in the early 1970s in Washington, D.C. to educate citizens on the "harmful effects" of abortion. It moved shortly thereafter to Chicago, where it could be closer to its dedicated cadre of supporters. Currently, AUL continues to publish materials advocating the right-to-life position, but its education and lobbying activities are implemented by its Legal Defense Fund, created in 1975 after *Roe.*

Americans United for Life Legal Defense Fund (AUL Legal Defense Fund). After the 1973 abortion decisions, anti-abortion groups became acutely aware of the utility of litigation. Although there are several groups that now represent the right-to-life position in the courts, the AUL Legal Defense Fund, which was founded in 1975, is the movement's only full-time public interest law firm.

Association Against the Prohibition Amendment (AAPA). The AAPA, supported by Irénée and Pierre du Pont, was formed to obtain repeal of the prohibition amendment. Leaders of the AAPA, including the du Ponts and Jouett Shouse, were instrumental in forming the American Liberty League, an anti-New Deal association.

Business Roundtable. The Roundtable was formed in Washington, D.C. in 1972 to act as a lobbying agent for the business community. Its membership includes chief executive officers from most major U.S. corporations. It provided the Equal Employment Advisory Council with money to publish *Comparable Worth*, which has been cited by the U.S. Supreme Court.

Capital Legal Foundation. The Capital Legal Foundation was created by the National Legal Center in Washington, D.C. in 1978. Since breaking with the center over a funding dispute, the Capital Legal Foundation currently considers itself an independent firm. Under the leadership of Dan Burt, the firm currently is representing General William Westmoreland in his suit against CBS.

Center for Law and Social Policy (CLASP). CLASP was founded in 1969 by Charles Halpern. It was one of the first liberal public interest law firms formed to handle a variety of cases ranging from environmental protection to media law and not just to specialize in one area of the law.

Center for Law in the Public Interest. The center was created in 1971 to bring the liberal version of the public interest to court. Its litigation has been broad in scope, ranging from environmental issues to civil rights. It is currently located in Los Angeles, California.

Center for the Study of Responsive Law. The center was originally established by Ralph Nader in 1968. Currently, it "encourages" public and private sector groups to consider the "needs of consumers."

Chamber of Commerce. The Chamber was established in 1912, at the request of President William Howard Taft, to provide a closer link between "commercial interests" and the federal government. Even though the Chamber has always been aware of the importance of court decisions, it was not until the late 1970s that it established the National Chamber Litigation Center specifically to litigate.

Christian American Association. The association was formed by a group of Houston businessmen after the Wagner Act was upheld in court. Financed by anti-union interests, the association lobbied for passage of anti-labor legislation in the states during the early 1940s.

Citizens for Decency through Law (CDL). CDL was established by Charles Keating, a member of the President's Commission on Obscenity, in 1957 to lobby for greater restrictions on obscenity. Since the Supreme Court began creating working definitions of obscenity, however, CDL has resorted to the courts in an attempt to fight to expand definitions and to ensure that obscenity convictions are sustained in the appellate courts.

Communications Workers of America (CWA). CWA was founded in 1938 and is currently a member of the AFL-CIO. Since the early 1970s CWA practices have been challenged in court by the National Right to Work Legal Defense Foundation.

Eagle Forum. The Eagle Forum was founded in 1975 by Phyllis Schlafly, who now serves as its president. The group lobbied against passage of the Equal Rights Amendment and is currently support-ing legislation that would legalize prayer in school.

Edison Electric Institute.   The institute was founded in 1933 to re-place the National Electric Light Association. Its initial purpose was to police the industry. When the electric industry was threatened by New Deal legislation, however, the institute quickly expanded the scope of its activities to include litigation to challenge the con-stitutionality of laws onerous to the industry.

Equal Employment Advisory Council (EEAC).   The EEAC was founded in 1976 by several attorneys, including members of the law firm of McGuiness and Williams. It participates solely as an ami-cus curiae in federal equal employment opportunity litigation.

Executive Committee of Southern Cotton Manufacturers.   The committee was formed in 1915 specifically to counter efforts being made on behalf of child labor legislation. Once these efforts proved unsuccessful on the legislative front, the committee turned imme-diately to litigation.

General Federation of Women's Clubs.   Formed at the turn of the century, the federation was an "umbrella" association for literary and civic women's clubs. It supported numerous progressive reforms, including passage of child labor laws.

Great Plains Legal Foundation.   Located in Kansas City, Missouri, the foundation was one of six firms established with the help of the National Legal Center. Its first president, Christopher Bond, was a former governor of Missouri and a head of the Chamber of Com-merce. In 1981 the Great Plains Legal Foundation and the Gulf Coast Legal Foundation merged because of problems they encountered while operating individually. In 1982 they were joined by another fledgling firm, the Legal Foundation of America.

Gulf Coast Legal Foundation.   Once an independent conservative public interest law firm, the foundation merged with a National Legal Center-affiliated firm, the Great Plains Legal Foundation, in 1981. The Gulf Coast and Great Plains Legal Foundation of America, as it is currently called, is located in Kansas City, Missouri.

Heritage Foundation. Founded in 1974, the Heritage Foundation is an important conservative "think tank." It has attempted to facilitate the development of a coherent conservative public interest law movement by holding monthly luncheons, attended by numerous conservative litigation groups.

International Association of Police Chiefs (IACP). Representing the interests of law-enforcement officials, the IACP was founded in 1893. Currently it participates as an amicus curiae in litigation involving criminal issues, often cosigning briefs filed by Americans for Effective Law Enforcement.

John Birch Society. Founded in 1958 by Robert Welch, the society is named after John Birch, a missionary killed in 1945 by the Chinese. It is noted for its conservative, anti-Communist stance and as such has lobbied for United States withdrawal from the United Nations and the eradication of federal regulatory agencies.

Legal Foundation of America. The foundation was created in Houston in 1980 by David Crump, a professor of law at the University of Houston, and his wife, Susan Crump, a former county assistant district attorney. In 1982 this conservative legal foundation merged with two other fledgling firms to create the Gulf Coast and Great Plains Legal Foundation of America.

Man Suffrage Association Opposed to Political Suffrage for Women. This association was established in 1912 by Everett Wheeler to stop ratification of the suffrage amendment. Later Wheeler created the American Constitutional League, which played a major role in progressive litigation.

Maryland League for State Defense. The league was formed in 1919 to preserve the concept of states' rights through litigation. Supported by prominent attorneys, it often acted in concert with other conservative groups.

Mid-America Legal Foundation. Charged with bringing the conservative definition of the public interest to the courts in the Midwest, the foundation is one of six firms created by the National Legal Center. It is currently located in Chicago, where it retains close ties to the business community.

Mid-Atlantic Legal Foundation. Located in Philadelphia, the foundation is one of six firms affiliated with the National Legal Center. It was created in 1978 and currently is headed by Myrna Field, the only woman leader of a conservative legal foundation.

Moral Majority. Founded by Jerry Falwell, the Moral Majority's purpose is to work for pro-God, pro-family policies. Since its formation, the Moral Majority has lobbied Congress for passage of such legislation and has worked for candidates who agree with its policies.

Mountain States Legal Foundation (MSLF). Under the leadership of Leonard Theberge, the National Legal Center facilitated the creation of the MSLF in Denver in 1978. MSLF's former president was James Watt, a secretary of the interior during the Reagan administration.

National Abortion Rights Action League (NARAL). Formerly called the National Association for the Repeal of Abortion Laws, NARAL was established in 1969 to lobby for repeal of restrictive state abortion statutes. It currently bills itself as "the largest single-issue, pro-choice organization" in the United States.

National Association for the Advancement of Colored People (NAACP). The NAACP was founded in 1909 by persons concerned over the pervasive discrimination faced by blacks. Since that time it has been at the forefront of efforts for change.

National Association for the Advancement of Colored People Legal Defense Fund (NAACP Legal Defense Fund). The Legal Defense Fund was created by the NAACP in 1939 specifically to use litigation as a weapon in the war against race discrimination. Currently, the Legal Defense Fund is completely independent of the NAACP and in fact in 1983 lost its right to use the NAACP name.

National Association of Manufacturers (NAM). NAM was organized in 1895 and like other employer associations of the day was defended by the Anti-Boycott Association in court. Today, NAM is an umbrella organization for numerous industrial companies.

National Association Opposed to Women Suffrage (NAOWS). NAOWS was founded in 1911 by women opposed to state and national women suffrage proposals. Although it did not engage in litigation, it did publicize and support litigation efforts of like-minded groups.

National Child Labor Committee. The committee was formed in 1904 to seek protections for children and in particular to obtain passage of a child labor amendment. Many of its leaders were also involved in the National Consumers' League.

National Committee for an Effective Congress. The committee was formed in 1948 to provide financing and advice to candidates. It supports candidates who will "advance the liberties and rights of all Americans."

National Conservative Political Action Committee (NCPAC). The NCPAC was founded in 1975 to collect and distribute money to conservative candidates. In 1980 the NCPAC took credit for the defeat of several high-ranking liberal U.S. senators. It currently claims to be the largest conservative PAC.

National Consumers' League. Founded at the turn of the century, the league was initially a coalition of several associations, all of which were formed by women concerned with working conditions for women and children. Although the group initially lobbied for passage of protective legislation, it soon took to the courts when employers challenged its legislation in court.

National District Attorneys Association (NDAA). Founded in 1950, the NDAA's membership consists of prosecuting attorneys throughout the United States. Currently, it participates as an amicus curiae mainly in litigation involving criminal issues, but its more recent briefs have been filed in conjunction with Americans for Effective Law Enforcement.

National Electric Light Association (NELA).   The NELA was established in 1885 by power companies to advance their interests. So controversial were its methods that it was reorganized under a new name, the Edison Electric Institute.

National Lawyers' Committee (NLC).   Founded in 1935 by leaders of the American Liberty League who believed that the public interest was best served when government avoided legislating on behalf of the "public," the NLC used litigation until its demise in 1940 to challenge all types of New Deal legislation.

National Legal Center for the Public Interest (NLCPI).   The NLCPI was established in 1975 by Leonard Theberge, who had been commissioned by the Pacific Legal Foundation to conduct a study on the need for more conservative legal foundations. Before the PLF could consider the advisability of Theberge's recommendation to create more firms, Theberge formed the NLCPI with the sole purpose of establishing a network of conservative firms. He eventually established six firms, whose activities NLCPI still claims to coordinate. Most of these firms now claim to be quite independent of the NLCPI, however.

National Right to Life Committee.   Founded in 1973, the committee calls itself "an international clearinghouse" for anti-abortion groups. Its current objectives include passage of a human life type of amendment.

National Right to Work Committee.   The committee was formed in 1955 to lobby for state right-to-work laws. It soon realized, however, that legislative lobbying could be supplemented by litigation. Therefore, in 1968 its leaders formed an independent legal defense foundation.

National Right to Work Legal Defense Foundation.   Modeled after the NAACP Legal Defense Fund, the foundation was created because the National Right to Work Committee was not "structured" to mount long-term litigation campaigns against compulsory union practices and union violence.

National Support Roosevelt League. The National Support Roosevelt League was created to support President Franklin Roosevelt's New Deal legislation. It also claimed responsibility for an American Bar Association inquiry into the activities of the National Lawyers' Committee, although this claim was later disproved.

New England Legal Foundation. The New England Legal Foundation is a conservative public interest law firm. Formed in 1976, the foundation has litigated in a variety of areas including environmental law, first amendment liberties, and government regulation. It is currently located in Boston.

Pacific Legal Foundation (PLF). The Pacific Legal Foundation was established in 1973 in Sacramento, by several members of then governor Ronald Reagan's administration, including Edwin Meese, who were alarmed by liberal groups' success in getting their definition of the public interest entrenched in the courts. As the first conservative public interest legal foundation, the PLF has attempted to bring its view of the public interest to the courts in a variety of issue areas, including environmental law, affirmative action, and property rights.

Planned Parenthood. Planned Parenthood was formed by birth-control advocate Margaret Sanger in 1916, making it the oldest "planning agency" in the United States. It, as well as its affiliates, have been involved in numerous reproductive freedom cases before the Supreme Court.

Public Advocates. Founded in 1971, Public Advocates is a liberal public interest law firm that concentrates on representing "disadvantaged" groups, including the poor, the elderly, and racial minorities. It has represented numerous organizations in court, such as the NAACP, the National Organization for Women, and Gray Panthers.

Public Citizen Litigation Group. Formed by Ralph Nader in 1972, the Public Citizen Litigation Group resorts to the courts in cases involving consumer issues. It has also done some litigation dealing with election laws.

Public Interest Research Group (PIRG). Formed in 1968 by Ralph Nader, PIRG bills itself as a "public interest" organization involved in consumer issues.

Sentinels of the Republic. The Sentinels were formed in Massachusetts in 1921. Its members were prominent anti-progressives who viewed litigation through test cases as the most important method to challenge progressive legislation.

Southeastern Legal Foundation (SELF). The Southeastern Legal Foundation was one of six firms the National Legal Center helped to establish. Located in Atlanta, SELF was headed by Ben Blackburn, a former member of Congress.

Victims' Assistance Legal Organization (VALOR). Formerly the Crime Victims' Legal Advocacy Institute, VALOR was initially created as part of Americans for Effective Law Enforcement by Frank Carrington, who had been the executive director of AELE. In 1980, however, VALOR became an independent organization, serving as a clearinghouse for victims' rights litigation.

Washington Legal Foundation (WLF). WLF was established by Dan Popeo in 1976 in Washington, D.C. to defend the free enterprise system and to counter the liberal public interest law movement. Since then, the WLF has been involved in numerous issues, including victims' rights, government regulation, and capital punishment. Most notably, it represented sixty-one members of Congress in their suit against what it called President Carter's "transfer" of the Panama Canal.

Women's Joint Congressional Committee (WJCC). The WJCC was founded in 1920 by women who had been active in the suffrage effort and wanted a way to continue to have influence on public policy. Composed of several leading women's groups of the day, it was the main mover behind passage of the Sheppard-Towner Maternity Act.

TABLE OF CASES

REFERENCES

America (April 1958). "Public Opinion Against Smut," 99:2.
———. (January 1959). "Bad Day for Dirty Books," 100:488.
American Bar Association. 1935. Committee on Professional Ethics and Grievances of the American Bar Association. Opinion no. 148.
American Federation of Labor. 1907. *American Federationist*, p. 784.
———. 1908. 28th Annual Convention of the AFL. Resolution no. 97.
Americans for Effective Law Enforcement. No date, a. Pamphlet.
———. No date, b. *"Impact."*
———. 1973. "Criminal Justice IMPACT."
———. (October 1975). Amicus curiae brief filed in *South Dakota v. Opperman*, no. 75–76.
———. (October 1980). Amicus curiae brief filed in *United States v. Ross*, no. 2209.
Americans United for Life. No date, a. Pamphlet.
———. No date, b. Pamphlet: *Defending the Cause of Life.*
———. (December 1977). *Lex Vitae*, p. 6.
———. (August 1978). *Lex Vitae*, p. 4.
———. (June 1979). *Lex Vitae*, p. 4.
———. (October 1975). Amicus curiae brief filed in *Planned Parenthood v. Danforth*, no. 74-1151.
———. (October 1976). Brief in opposition to motion to dismiss or affirm appeals in *Califano v. McRae*, no. 76-694.
———. (October 1980). Amicus curiae brief filed in *H.L. v. Matheson*, no. 79-5903.
Anderson, Frederick R. 1973. *NEPA in the Courts*. Baltimore: Johns Hopkins Univ. Press.
Angell, Ernest. 1967. "The Amicus Curiae: American Development of an English Institution." *International and Comparative Law Quarterly* 16: 1017–44.

Balides, Constance, et al. 1973. "The Abortion Issue: Major Groups." In *The Abortion Experience*, ed. Howard and Joy Osofsky. Baltimore: Harper & Row.

Ball, Howard. 1980. *Courts and Politics: The Federal Judicial System.* Englewood Cliffs, N.J.: Prentice-Hall.

Baker, Stewart A., and James R. Asperger. 1982. "Forward: Toward a Center for State and Local Legal Advocacy." *Catholic University Law Review* 31:367–373.

Barker, Lucius. 1967. "Third Parties in Litigation: A Systematic View of Judicial Function." *Journal of Politics* 29:41–69.

Barker, Lucius, and Twiley Barker. 1965. *Freedom, Courts and Politics.* Englewood Cliffs, N.J.: Prentice-Hall.

———. 1982. *Civil Liberties and the Constitution — Cases and Comment.* 4th ed. Englewood Cliffs, N.J.: Prentice-Hall.

Baron, Stanley. 1962. *Brewed in America — A History of Beer and Ale in the United States.* Boston: Little, Brown.

Baum, Lawrence. 1981. *The Supreme Court.* Washington, D.C.: Congressional Quarterly.

Bean, Barton. 1955. "Pressure for Freedom: The American Civil Liberties Union." Ph.D. diss., Cornell Univ.

Beckwith, Edmund, and Rudolph Sobernheim. 1948. "Amicus Curiae — Minister of Justice." *Fordham Law Review* 17:38–62.

Bell, Griffin B. 1982. *Taking Care of the Law.* New York: Morrow.

Belton, Robert. 1978. "A Comparative Review of Public and Private Enforcement of Title VII of the Civil Rights Act of 1964." *Vanderbilt Law Review* 31:905–61.

Bendeck, Odette. 1982. "Assessing the Impact of Amicus Curiae Briefs: A Case Study of the Effectiveness of the Equal Employment Advisory Council's Amicus Curiae Strategy." Honors thesis, Emory Univ.

Bentley, Arthur. 1908. *The Process of Government.* Chicago: Univ. of Chicago Press.

Berger, Margaret A. 1979. "Litigation on Behalf of Women: An Assessment." Mimeo. Ford Foundation.

Berns, Walter F. 1957. *Freedom, Virtue, and the First Amendment.* Baton Rouge: Louisiana State Univ. Press.

Berry, Jeffrey M. 1977. *Lobbying for the People: The Political Behavior of Public Interest Groups.* Princeton, N.J.: Princeton Univ. Press.

Birkby, Robert H., and Walter Murphy. 1964. "Interest Group Conflict in the Judicial Arena." *Texas Law Review* 42:1018–48.

Black, Henry Campbell. 1968. *Black's Law Dictionary.* 4th ed. St. Paul, Minn.: West.

Blaisdell, Donald. 1957. *American Democracy Under Pressure.* New York: Ronald.

Blumberg, Dorothy Rose. 1966. *Florence Kelley: The Making of a Social Pioneer.* New York: Kelley.

Bonnett, Clarence. 1922. *Employers' Associations in the United States: A Study of Typical Associations.* New York: Macmillan.

Broder, David. 1980. *Changing of the Guard*. Middlesex, Eng.: Penguin Books.

Brophy, Beth. (21 January 1980). "Defenders of the Right." *Forbes* 125: 84–86.

Business Week (25 January 1933). "Utility Ethics," p. 12.

――――. (10 November 1980). "A Business Group Fights 'Comparable Worth,'" p. 100.

Burke, Susan Olson. 1981. "The Political Evolution of Interest Group Litigation." In *Governing Through Courts*, ed. Richard A.L. Gambritta et al. Beverly Hills: Sage.

Burt, Dan M. 1982. *Abuse of Trust – A Report on Ralph Nader's Network*. Chicago: Regnery Gateway.

Califano, Joseph A. 1981. *Governing America – An Insider's Report from the White House and the Cabinet*. New York: Simon and Schuster.

Cameron, Bruce. 1982. Staff Attorney, National Right to Work Legal Defense Foundation. Interview with author.

Carrington, Frank C. 1975. *The Victims*. New Rochelle, N.Y.: Arlington House.

Cass, Ronald A., and Charles J. Goetz. No date. "Public Interest Law and the Business-Oriented Legal Foundation: Overcoming Externalities." Manuscript.

Cates, Willard. 1981. "The Hyde Amendment in Action." *Journal of the American Medical Association* 246:1109–12.

Catt, Carrie Chapman, and Nettie Rogers Shuler. 1969. *Woman Suffrage and Politics – The Inner Story of the Suffrage Movement*. New York: Scribner.

Charen, Mona (10 December 1982). "Going Courting in Washington." *National Review* 240:1554–55.

Chase, Harold W. 1972. *Federal Judges*. Minneapolis, Minn.: Univ. of Minnesota Press.

Childs, Harwood Lawrence. 1930. *Labor and Capital in National Politics*. Columbus, Ohio: Ohio State Univ. Press.

Citizens for Decency Through Law. October 1981. Amicus curiae brief filed in *New York v. Ferber*, no. 81–53.

――――. No date. Pamphlet.

Clark, Timothy B. (12 July 1980). "After a Decade of Doing Battle, Public Interest Groups Show Their Age." *National Journal* 28:1136–41.

Cook, Constance Ewing. 1980. *Nuclear Power and Legal Advocacy: The Environmentalists and the Courts*. Lexington, Mass: Lexington.

Corey, Frank, Jr. 1959. "Amicus Curiae: Friend of the Court." *De Paul Law Review* 9:30–37.

Cortner, Richard C. 1964. *The Wagner Act Cases*. Knoxville: Univ. of Tennessee Press.

――――. 1968. "Strategies and Tactics of Litigants in Constitutional Cases." *Journal of Public Law* 17:287–307.

――――. 1970a. *The Jones & Laughlin Case*. New York: Knopf.

————. 1970b. *The Apportionment Cases.* Knoxville: Univ. of Tennessee Press.

Cortner, Richard C., and Clifford M. Lytle. 1971. *Modern Constitutional Law: Commentary and Cases.* New York: Free Press.

————. 1975. *The Supreme Court and Civil Liberties Policy.* Palo Alto, Calif.: Mayfield.

————. 1980. *The Supreme Court and the Second Bill of Rights.* Madison: Univ. of Wisconsin Press.

Corwin, Edwin S. 1920. "Constitutional Law in 1919–1920." *American Political Science Review* 14:633–58.

Costain, Anne. 1980. "The Struggle for a National Women's Lobby: Organizing a Diffuse Interest." *Western Political Quarterly* 33:476–91.

Council for Public Interest Law. 1976. *Balancing the Scales of Justice: Financing Public Interest Law in America.* The Council for Public Interest Law.

Cowan, Ruth B. 1976. "Women's Rights Through Litigation: An Examination of the American Civil Liberties Union Women's Rights Project, 1971–1976." *Columbia Human Rights Law Review* 8:373–412.

Craemer, Kevin J. 1981. Membership coordinator, National District Attorneys Association. Correspondence with author.

Crawford, Alan. 1980. *Thunder on the Right.* New York: Pantheon.

Cumberland Law Review. 1976. "Quasi-Party in the Guise of Amicus Curiae," 7:293–305.

de Toledano, Ralph. 1974. "Joe Rauh's Counterattack." *National Review* 26:1461–63.

————. 1975. *Hit and Run. The Rise and Fall? of Ralph Nader.* New Rochelle, N.Y.: Arlington Books.

Dorsen, Norman. 1968. *Frontiers of Civil Liberties.* New York: Pantheon.

Dubois, Ellen Carol. 1978. *Feminism and Suffrage – The Emergence of An Independent Women's Movement in America, 1848–1869.* Ithaca, N.Y.: Cornell Univ. Press.

Duggan, Linda J. (10 May 1982). Associate Director, Victims Assistance Legal Organization. Correspondence with author.

Dye, Thomas R., and L. Harmon Zeigler. 1983. *American Politics in the Media Age.* Monterey, Calif.: Brooks/Cole.

Epstein, Lee. 1982. "Interest Groups, Controversy, and the Court: An Analysis of Abortion Litigation." Master's thesis, Emory Univ.

Equal Employment Advisory Commission. 1981. *Comparable Worth: Issues and Alternatives.*

————. 1982. *Annual Report.*

Flexner, Eleanor. 1974. *Century of Struggle – The Women's Rights Movement in the U.S.* New York: Atheneum.

Ford Foundation. 1973. *The Public Interest Law Firms – New Voices for New Constituencies.* New York: Ford Foundation.

————. 1977. *Nine for Equality Under Law – Civil Rights Litigation.* New York: Ford Foundation.

Frank, John P. 1972. *Marble Palace – The Supreme Court in American Life.*
New York: Knopf.

Freeman, Jo. 1975. *The Politics of Women's Liberation.* New York: David
McKay.

Freund, Paul A. 1949. *On Understanding the Supreme Court.* Boston: Little, Brown.

Funston, Richard Y. 1977. *Constitutional Counterrevolution: The Warren
Court and the Burger Court and Judicial Policy-Making in Modern America.* New York: Schenkman.

Galanter, Marc. 1974. "Why the 'Haves' Come Out Ahead: Speculation
on the Limits of Legal Change." *Law and Society Review* 9:95–160.

Gelb, Joyce, and Marian Lief Palley. 1982. *Women and Public Policies.*
Princeton, N.J.: Princeton Univ. Press.

Gerber, Albert B. 1965. *Sex, Pornography, and Justice.* New York: Lyle
Stuart.

Ginger, Ann Fagan. 1963. "Litigation as a Form of Political Action."
Wayne Law Review 9:458–83.

Goldman, Sheldon. 1967. "Judicial Appointments to the United States
Courts of Appeals." *Wisconsin Law Review,* 186–214.

———. 1982. *Constitutional Law and Supreme Court Decision-Making.*
New York: Harper & Row.

Goldman, Sheldon, and Austin Sarat, eds. 1978. *American Court Systems.*
San Francisco: Freeman.

Goldmark, Josephine. 1953. *Impatient Crusader: Florence Kelley's Life
Story.* Urbana: Univ. of Illinois Press.

Graham, Fred P. (21 February 1972). "A Counterweight to A.C.L.U.
Thrives." *New York Times* 26:6.

Gray, Robert T. 1978. "A New Day in Court for Business." *National
Business* 66:26–29.

Greenberg, Jack. 1974. "Litigation for Social Change: Methods, Limits,
and Role in Democracy." *Records of the New York City Bar Association*
29:9–63.

———. 1976. "The Death Penalty: Where Do We Go from Here?" *NLADA
Briefcase* 34:55–57.

———. 1977. *Judicial Process and Social Change: Constitutional Litigation.* St. Paul, Minn.: West.

Greenwald, Carol S. 1975. "The Use of Litigation by Common Cause: A
Study of the Development of Campaign Finance Reform Legislation."
Paper presented to the American Political Science Association, San
Francisco.

———. 1977. *Group Power: Lobbying and Public Policy.* New York:
Praeger.

———. 1978. "Women's Rights, Courts and Congress: Conflict Over Pregnancy Disability Compensation Policies." Paper presented to the American Political Science Association, New York.

Grossman, Joel B. 1965. *Lawyers and Judges: The ABA and the Politics of
Judicial Selection.* New York: Wiley.

Group Research. (28 January 1974). p. 2.

Hahn, Jeanne. 1973. "The NAACP Legal Defense and Educational Fund: Its Judicial Strategy and Tactics." In *American Government and Politics*, ed. Stephen L. Wasby. New York: Scribner.

Hakman, Nathan. 1966. "Lobbying the Supreme Court: An Appraisal of Political Science 'Folklore.'" *Fordham Law Review* 35:15–50.

―――. 1969. "The Supreme Court's Political Environment: The Processing of Noncommercial Litigation." In *Frontiers of Judicial Research*, ed. Joel B. Grossman and Joseph Tanenhaus. New York: Wiley.

Hall, Charles. 1964. "Poison in Print—And How to Get Rid of It." *Reader's Digest* 84:94–98.

Hall, Donald. 1969. *Cooperative Lobbying—The Power of Pressure.* Tucson: Univ. of Arizona Press.

Halloran, Richard. 1970a. "Federal Commission on Pornography Now Divided on the Easing of Controls." *New York Times* 42:1:8.

―――. 1970b. "Dissenter Seeks Smut Report Bar." *New York Times* 8:1.

Halpern. Charles R. 1974. "Public Interest Law: Its Past and Future." *Judicature* 58:118–27.

Halpern, Charles R., and John M. Cunningham. 1971. "Reflections on the New Public Interest Law: Theory and Practice at the Center for Law and Social Policy." *Georgetown Law Journal* 59:1095–121.

Halpern, Stephen C. 1976. "Assessing the Litigative Role of ACLU Chapters." In *Civil Liberties: Policy and Policy Making*, ed. Stephen L. Wasby. Lexington, Mass.: Lexington.

Handler, Joel. 1978a. *Social Movements and the Legal System.* New York: Academic Press.

―――. 1978b. "The Public Interest Law Industry." In *Public Interest Law: An Economic and Institutional Analysis*, ed. Burton A. Weisbrod. Berkeley, California: University of California Press.

Harper, Fowler V., and Edwin D. Etherington. 1952. "Lobbyists Before the Court." *University of Pennsylvania Law Review* 101:1172–77.

Harris, Richard. 1971. *Decision.* New York: Dutton.

Harrison, Gordon, and Sanford Jaffe. 1973. *The Public Interest Law Firm.* New York: Ford Foundation.

Herring, Pendleton. 1929. *Group Representation Before Congress.* Baltimore: Johns Hopkins Univ. Press.

Hole, Judith, and Ellen Levine. 1971. *Rebirth of Feminism.* New York: Quadrangle.

Horowitz, Michael J. 1980. "The Public Interest Law Movement: Analysis with Special Reference to the Role and Practices of Conservative Public Interest Law for Scaife." Mimeo. Scaife Foundation.

―――. 1981. "In Defense of Public Interest Law." In *Perspectives on Public Interest Law.* New York: Institute for Educational Affairs.

―――. 1983. Chief Legal Officer, Office of Management and Budget. Interview with author.

Hueter, Ernest. 1982. President, National Legal Center for the Public Interest. Interview with author.

Hull, Kent. 1978. "Advocates as Amicus Curiae: Friends of the Court Effect Change." *Amicus* 3:27–30.

Ippolito, Dennis S., and Thomas A. Walker. 1980. *Political Parties, Interest Groups, and Public Policy: Group Influence in American Politics.* Englewood Cliffs, N.J.: Prentice-Hall.

Irons, Peter H. 1982. *The New Deal Lawyers.* Princeton, N.J.: Princeton Univ. Press.

Jacob, Herbert. 1978. *Justice in America.* Boston: Little, Brown.

Jaffe, Sanford. 1976. *Public Interest Law: Five Years Later.* New York: Ford Foundation.

Johnson, Donald. 1963. *The Challenge to American Freedom.* Lexington: Univ. of Kentucky Press.

Johnson, Willa. 1983. Resource Bank Director, Heritage Foundation. Interview with author.

Jones, Emma Coleman. 1979. "Litigation Without Representation: The Need for Intervention to Affirmative Action Litigation." *Harvard Civil Rights-Civil Liberties* 14: 31–87.

———. 1980. "Problems and Prospects of Participation in Affirmative Action Litigation: A Role for Intervenors." *University of California, Davis Law Review* 13:221–29.

Jordan, Ellen R., and Paul H. Rubin. 1981. "Government Regulation and Economic Efficiency: The Role of Conservative Legal Foundations." In *A Blueprint for Judicial Reform,* ed. Patrick B. McGuigan and Randall R. Nader. Washington, D.C.: Free Congress Research and Education Foundation.

Judiciary Committee of the United States Senate. July 1968. "Nomination of Abe Fortas to be Chief Justice of the United States Supreme Court." Pt. 1.

Junk, Howard. 1965. "Smut Hunters—The New Jurisprudency." *Nation* 201:358–60.

Katz, Ellis. 1967. "The Supreme Court in the Web of Government: The ACLU, the Supreme Court and the Bible." Ph.D. diss., Columbia University.

Keller, Morton. 1958. *In Defense of Yesterday—James M. Beck and the Politics of Conservatives.* New York: Coward-McCann.

Kellogg, Charles. 1967. NAACP: A History of the National Association for the Advancement of Colored People.* Baltimore: Johns Hopkins Univ. Press.

Key, V. O. 1964. *Politics, Parties and Pressure Groups.* New York: Crowell.

Kluger, Richard. 1976. *Simple Justice: The History of Brown v. Board of Education and Black Americans' Struggle for Equality.* New York: Knopf.

Krislov, Samuel. 1963. "The Amicus Curiae Brief: From Friendship to Advocacy." *Yale Law Journal* 72:694–721.

Kristol, Irving. 1981. "Public Interest Law: An Overview." In *Perspectives on Public Interest Law.* New York: Institute for Educational Affairs.

Kyvig, David E. 1979. *Repealing National Prohibition.* Chicago: Univ. of Chicago Press.

Lader, Lawrence. 1973. *Abortion II*. Boston: Beacon Press.

Lee, Rex E. 1982. Solicitor General of the United States. Interview with Karen O'Connor.

Levin, Betsy, and Phillip Moise. 1975. "School Desegregation Litigation in the Seventies and the Use of Social Science Evidence: An Annotated Guide." *Law and Contemporary Problems* 39:50–134.

Lewis, Anthony (3 December 1963). "High Court Backs Rights of States in Curbing Unions." *New York Times* 1:8.

Lieberman, Elias. 1950. *Unions Before the Bar — Historical Trials Showing the Evolution of Labor Rights in the United States*. New York: Harper.

Liroff, Richard. 1977. NEPA *and Its Aftermath: The Formation of a National Policy for the Environment*. Bloomington, Ind.: Indiana Univ. Press.

McCaughey, John. (11 January 1980). "A New Public for Public Interest." Reprinted by the Washington Legal Foundation from *The Energy Daily*.

McCommon, Paul. 1983. Staff Attorney, Citizens for Decency through Law. Telephone conversation with author.

McDonald, Michael P. 1982. "Natural Gas: The Necessity of Deregulation." Washington, D.C.: Washington Legal Foundation.

McDowell, Douglas S. 1982. Staff Attorney, Equal Employment Advisory Council. Interview with author.

Manwaring, David. 1962. *Render Unto Caesar: The Flag Salute Controversy*. Chicago: Univ. of Chicago Press.

Marcus, Ruth. (5 August 1982). "Court Watch Group Puts Pressure on 'Lenient Judges.'" *Washington Post* 8:1–4.

Mark, Norman. (5 July 1965). "Censorship: Fanatics and Fallacies." *Nation* 201:5–7.

Markmann, Charles. 1965. *The Noblest Cry*. New York: St. Martin's Press.

Marshall, Thurgood. 1969. "Group Action in the Pursuit of Justice." *New York University Law Review* 44:661–72.

Marzen, Thomas. 1983. Staff Attorney, Americans United for Life Legal Defense Fund. Interview with author.

Maslow, Will. 1955. "The Use of Law in the Struggle for Equality." *Social Research* 22:297–314.

———. 1961. "The Legal Defense of Religious Liberty — The Strategy and Tactics of the American Jewish Congress." Paper presented to the American Political Science Association.

Meier, August, and Elliot Rudwick. 1976. "Attorneys Black and White: A Case of Race Relations within the NAACP." *Journal of American History* 62:913–46.

Mellor, William. 1982. Staff Attorney, Mountain States Legal Foundation. Interview with Karen O'Connor.

Meltsner, Michael. 1973. *Cruel and Unusual: The Supreme Court and Capital Punishment*. New York: Random House.

Merritt, Walter Gordon. 1970. *History of the League for Industrial Rights*. New York: Da Capa.

Merton, Andrew H. 1981. *Enemies of Choice — The Right-To-Life Movement and Its Threat to Abortion.* Boston: Beacon.

Mexican American Legal Defense and Educational Fund. No date. *Diez Años.*

Miller, Loren. 1966. *The Petitioner: The Study of the Supreme Court of the United States and the Negro.* Cleveland: World Publishing.

Momboisse, Raymond M. 1980a. "Public Interest Law — Plague or Panacea?" Paper delivered at the University of Wisconsin Law School.

———. 1980b. "The New Wave of Public Interest Law." Paper delivered at Georgetown University.

———. 1982. Managing Attorney, Pacific Legal Foundation. Interview with author.

Moore, Elizabeth. 1981. Administrative Secretary, National Right to Life Committee. Correspondence with author.

Morgan, Richard E. 1968. *The Politics of Religious Conflict: Church and State in America.* New York: Pegasus.

Murphy, Bruce Allen. 1982. *The Brandeis-Frankfurter Connection.* New York: Oxford Univ. Press.

Murphy, Walter F. 1959. "The South Counter-Attacks: The anti-NAACP Law." *Western Political Quarterly* 12:371–90.

Murphy, Walter F., and C. Herman Pritchett. 1979. "Interest Groups and Litigation." In *Courts, Judges and Politics,* ed. Walter F. Murphy and C. Herman Pritchett. New York: Random House.

Nagel, Charles. 1912. "A National Chamber of Commerce." *Harper's Weekly* 56:9.

Nathan, Maude. 1926. *The Story of an Epoch-Making Movement.* New York: Doubleday.

National Chamber Litigation Center. 1980–81. *Annual Report 1980–81.*

———. No date. Pamphlet: *Business Is Our Only Client.*

———. Fall 1981. *The Business Advocate* 3.

National Lawyers' Committee. 1935. *Report on the Constitutionality of the NLRA.* Pittsburgh: Smith.

———. October 1935. "The Duty of the Lawyer in the Present Crisis." Pamphlet no. 69.

———. November 1935. "The National Lawyers' Committee of the American Liberty League." Pamphlet no. 74.

National Legal Center for the Public Interest. 1980. *1980 Annual Report.*

National Right to Work Legal Defense Foundation. No date. Pamphlet.

———. 1979. *Annual Report 1979.*

———. 1980. *Annual Report 1980.*

———. 1981. *Annual Report — Celebrating a Year of National Recognition.*

———. October 1974. Petition for writ of certiorari in *National Right to Work v. United Auto Workers et al.,* no. 74-645.

Neier, Aryeh. 1979. *Defending My Enemy.* New York: Dutton.

Newland, Chester A. 1959. "Legal Periodicals and the Supreme Court." *Midwest Journal of Political Science* 3:58–74.

Newsweek. (4 December 1972). "The Other Side," 31–32.
New York Times. (9 April 1914). "Boycott Injunction Asked to Curb Union," 12:1.
———. (10 April 1914). "Federal Warning to Union Fight," 18:1.
———. (17 June 1914). "Attacks Anti-Trust Bill," 11:5.
———. (28 June 1914). "Government Trails Labor Union Trust," 11:5.
———. (15 January 1916). "Anti-Boycott Men Held," 7:5.
———. (5 January 1918). "Plead for Defending Fight on Suffrage," 10:5.
———. (5 June 1918). "Constitutional League to Disband," 9:3.
———. (6 September 1920). "To Fight Suffrage on Tennessee Note," 7:1.
———. (22 September 1920). "Move to Dismiss 'Antis' Appeal," 1:5.
———. (15 December 1920). "Test Suffrage Amendment," 14:7.
———. (21 January 1922). "Replies to Suffrage Suit," 12:7.
———. (24 January 1922). "Testing Validity of Suffrage Amendment," 14:8.
———. (25 January 1922). "End Suffrage Argument," 7:2.
———. (28 February 1922). "Woman's Suffrage Amendment Valid," 9:1.
———. (9 December 1923). "Sentinels Watch Law," 2:1.
———. (1 December 1924). "Sentinels to Confer on Child Labor Issue," 2:5.
———. (9 March 1928). "Defend Injunction Right," 13:2.
———. (23 June 1929). "Prominent Attorneys Open War on Dry Law," 2:5.
———. (25 April 1929). "Anti Dry Lawyers Expand Campaign," 12:2.
———. (14 June 1929). "Urges Bar to Lead in Dry Act Repeal," 24:8.
———. (24 October 1929). "Pledges to Halt Lawless Officials," 60:2.
———. (2 August 1931). "Lawyers Campaign Against Dry South," 2:6.
———. (28 November 1932). "Legalizing of Beer But Not Wine Urged," 1:5.
———. (13 January 1933). "Power Chiefs from National Institute to Purge Institute," 1:3.
———. (9 November 1933). "Lawyers' Wet Group Quits," 2:3.
———. (23 August 1934). "League Is Formed to Secure New Deal 'Protect Rights,'" 1:3.
———. (29 August 1934). "Pledges Power Is at Liberty League," 2:1.
———. (3 December 1934). "TVA Test Is Welcomed," 31:6.
———. (8 December 1934). "President Confers on Power Attack," 1:3.
———. (18 December 1934). "Federal Board Rebuffs Utility Request to Join Test of Validity," 1:1.
———. (22 August 1935). "Bar Group Studies Constitutionality of New Deal Acts," 1:3.
———. (24 August 1935). "Lawyer Group Scans New Deal Measure," 3:6.
———. (6 September 1935). "Shouse Back, Ready for 'Liberty' Fight," 19:4.
———. (13 September 1935). "Wagner Act Void, Legal Critics Hold," 1:3.
———. (13 September 1935). "Lead Fight for Utilities," 8:3.
———. (19 September 1935). "58 Lawyers Hold Labor Act Void," 1:3.
———. (17 October 1935). "Offers Free Defense of Citizens Rights," 6:4.
———. (30 October 1935). "Bar Asked to Oust Liberty League 58," 44:4.
———. (1 November 1935). "Says He Led Attack on Liberty League," 19:5.
———. (18 November 1935). "Bar Clears Group in Liberty League," 15:6.
———. (15 April 1936). "Links Labor 'Spies' to Liberty League," 7:1.

———. (24 September 1940). "New Deal Foe Folds Up," 20:3.

———. (5 July 1959). "Committee to Push 'Right to Work' Bill," 46:5.

———. (12 February 1962). "Union-Shop Foe Scored in Congress," 16:6.

———. (23 November 1967). "High Court Scored over Porno," 3:3.

———. (15 September 1970). "Panelists Agree on Smut Report," 23:3.

———. (24 January 1973). "US Court Rules Buckley Need Not Join TV Union," 83:1.

Northwestern Comment. 1960. "The Amicus Curiae." *Northwestern Law Review* 55:469–82.

Obscenity Report. 1971. *Obscenity Report*. London: Olympia.

O'Connor, Karen. 1980. *Women's Organizations' Use of the Courts*. Lexington, Mass: Lexington.

O'Connor, Karen, and Lee Epstein. 1982a. "Research Note: An Appraisal of Hakman's 'Folklore.'" *Law and Society Review* 16:701–11.

———. 1982b. "The Importance of Interest Group Involvement in Employment Discrimination Litigation." *Howard Law Journal* 23:301–21.

———. 1983a. "The Rise of Conservative Interest Group Litigation." *Journal of Politics* 45:479–89.

———. 1983b. "Beyond Legislative Lobbying: Women's Rights Groups and the Supreme Court." *Judicature* 67:134–43.

———. 1983c. "Court Rules and Workload: A Case Study of Rules Governing Amicus Curiae Participation." *The Justice System Journal* 8:35–45.

Odegard, Peter H. 1928. *Pressure Politics: The Study of the Anti Saloon League*. New York: Columbia Univ. Press.

O'Neill, Timothy J. 1980. "Advocacy Politics in *Bakke*: The Lawyer as Organizational Leader." Paper presented to the Northeast Political Science Association, New Haven.

Ornstein, Norman J., and Shirley Elder. 1978. *Interest Group Lobbying and Policy Making*. Washington, D.C.: Congressional Quarterly.

Osborne, George. 1963. "The NAACP in Alabama." In *The Third Branch of Government*, ed. C. Herman Pritchett and Alan Westin. New York: Harcourt, Brace, and World.

Pacific Legal Foundation. 1979–80. *Annual Report*.

———. 1980–81. *Eighth Annual Report*.

———. 1980. *Fact Sheet*.

———. 1980–81. *The Reporter*.

———. 1981–82. *Annual Report*.

Papachristou, Judith. 1976. *Women Together—A History in Documents of the Women's Movement*. New York: Knopf.

Paul, James N., and Murray Schwartz. 1961. *Federal Censorship: Obscenity in the Mail*. New York: Free Press.

Peltason, Jack. 1955. *Federal Courts in the Political Process*. New York: Random.

Pfeffer, Leo. 1981. "Amici in Church-State Litigation." *Law and Contemporary Problems* 44:83–110.

Piper, George C. 1967. "Amicus Curiae Participation—At the Court's Discretion." *Kentucky Law Journal* 55:864–73.

Pollitt, Daniel H. (October 1973). "Union Security in America." *American Federationist* 16–22.

Pomfret, John D. (12 October 1963). "Anti-Union Group Sued on Reports." *New York Times* 23:1.

Popeo, Daniel J. (March 1981). "Public Interest Law in the 1980s." *Barrons*, 278.

———. 1983. General Counsel, Washington Legal Foundation. Interview with author.

Potts, Malcom, et al. 1977. *Abortion*. Cambridge, Eng: Cambridge Univ. Press.

Powell, Lewis. 1971. "Attack on American Free System." Address before the Chamber of Commerce, quoted in Jack Greenberg "Litigation for Social Change: Methods, Limits and Role in Democracy." *Record of the New York City Bar Association* 29.

Pratt, Henry J. 1974. "Old Age Associations in National Politics." *Annals of the American Academy of Political and Social Science* 414:106–19.

Pritchett, C. Herman. 1941. "Divisions of Opinion Among Justices of the U.S. Supreme Court, 1939–1941." *American Political Science Review* 35: 890–98.

———. 1968. "Public Law and Judicial Behavior." *Journal of Politics* 30: 480–509.

Puro, Steven. 1971. "The Role of Amicus Curiae in the United States Supreme Court: 1920–1966." Ph.D. diss., State Univ. of New York at Buffalo.

Quinn, Tony. 1980. "Practicing Public Interest Law the Conservative Way." Reprinted by the Pacific Legal Foundation from *Western Law Journal*.

Rabin, Robert L. 1976. "Lawyers for Social Change: Perspectives on Public Interest Law." *Stanford Law Review* 28:207–61.

Reed, Rex. 1982. Interview with author. Legal Director, National Right to Work Legal Defense Foundation.

Rees, John. (10 November 1982). "Conservative Legal Advocate — Daniel J. Popeo." *The Review of the News*.

Reitman, Alan, ed. 1975. *The Pulse of Freedom*. New York: Norton.

Rembar, Charles. 1968. *The End of Obscenity*. New York: Random.

Rheingold, Paul D. 1965. "Mass Litigation Affecting Many Persons," *Trial* 2:29–32.

Rhett, R. Goodwyn. 1917. "No Peace While 'Kultor' Menaces." *Nation's Business*, p. 47.

Richardson, Richard, and Kenneth Vines. 1970. *The Politics of the Federal Courts*. Boston: Little, Brown.

Root, Grace C. 1934. *Women and Repeal*. New York: Harper.

Rosen, Paul L. 1972. *The Supreme Court and Social Science*. Urbana: Univ. of Illinois Press.

Rosenbaum, Walter A. 1973. *The Politics of Environmental Concern*. New York: Praeger.

Rubin, Eva. 1982. *Abortion, Politics and the Courts*. Westport, Conn.: Greenwood.

Rudolph, Frederick. 1950. "The American Liberty League, 1934–1940," *American Historical Review* 56:19–33.

Sanders, Joseph, et al. 1982. "The Relevance of 'Irrelevant' Testimony: Why Lawyers Use Social Science Experts in School Desegregation Cases." *Law and Society Review* 16:403–28.

Schmidt, Wayne M. 1981. Executive Director, Americans for Effective Law Enforcement. Correspondence with author.

Schmitt, Richard B. (21 August 1979). "Alternative Public Interest Law Firms Spring Up with Nader et al. as Target." *Wall Street Journal* 14: 1–2.

Schubert, Glendon. 1962. "The 1960 Term of the Supreme Court: A Psychological Analysis." *American Political Science Review* 56:90–107.

Scigliano, Robert. 1971. *The Supreme Court and the Presidency.* New York: Free Press.

Shapiro, David L. 1968. "Some Thoughts on Intervention Before Courts, Agencies, and Arbitrators." *Harvard Law Review* 8:721–72.

Shattuck, Petra T., and Jill Norgren. 1979. "Political Use of the Legal Process by Blacks and American Indian Minorities." *Howard Law Journal* 22:1.

Sherwood, Peter. 1981. Staff Attorney, NAACP Legal Defense Fund. Interview with author.

Shields, Geoffrey, and Sanford Spector. 1972. "Opening Up the Suburbs: Notes on a Movement for Social Change." *Yale Review of Law and Social Action* 2:330–33.

Sibley, Harper. 1937. "Business Looking Ahead." *Nation's Business* 25: 35–37.

Silberman, Laurence H. 1981. "Public Interest vs. Judicial Restraint." In *Perspectives on Public Interest Law.* New York: Institute for Educational Affairs.

Singer, James W. 1979. "Liberal Public Interest Law Firms Face Budgetary, Ideological Challenges." *National Journal* 2052–56.

Sklar, Zachary. 1979. "The Right to Work Lobby." *Nation* 228:33.

Smith, Robert. (30 October 1971). "Panel Suggested to Monitor FBI." *New York Times* 13:3.

———. (11 November 1971a). "A $70,000 Study of FBI Commissioned by Group Backing Bureau." *New York Times* 27:1.

Snow, A., and Burton Weisbrod. 1978. "Consumerism, Consumers and Public Interest Law." In *Public Interest Law: An Economic and Institutional Analysis,* ed. Burton Weisbrod. Berkeley: Univ. of California Press.

Sorauf, Frank J. 1957. "The Public Interest Reconsidered." *Journal of Politics* 19:616–39.

———. 1976. *The Wall of Separation: Constitutional Politics of Church and State.* Princeton, N.J.: Princeton Univ. Press.

Southern California Law Review. 1972. "The Tax-Exempt Status of Public Interest Law Firms," 45:228–48.

Stein, Barbara A. 1976. "Public Interest Law: The Balancing Act." *Trial* 12:12–14.

Stern, Robert, and Eugene Gressman. 1978. *Supreme Court Practice.* Washington, D.C.: Bureau of National Affairs.

Stewart, Joseph Jr., and Edward Heck. 1982. "Ensuring Access to Justice: the Role of Interest Group Lawyers in the 6os Campaign for Civil Rights." *Judicature* 66:84–95.

Strobel, Lee (6 July 1980). "Pro-Life Group Commands Respect." *Chicago Tribune*, p. 6.

Sturges, Kenneth. 1915. *American Chambers of Commerce.* New York: Moffat, Bard.

Taylor, Albion Guilford. 1961. *Labor and the Supreme Court.* Ann Arbor, Mich.: Braun-Brumfield.

Taylor, Stuart, Jr. (22 April 1982). "Conservative 'Public Interest Law' Firms Emerge." *New York Times*, p. 16.

Tenofsky, Elliot. 1980. "Interest Groups and Litigation: The Commission on Law and Social Action of the American Jewish Congress." Ph.D. diss., Brandeis University.

Terris, Bruce J. 1974. "Hard Times Ahead for Public Interest Law." *Juris Doctor* 4:22–29.

Timberlake, James H. 1963. *Prohibition and the Progressive Movement – 1900–1920.* Cambridge, Mass.: Harvard Univ. Press.

Time (May 1973). "Donors for Suits," 101:76.

Trubek, David M. 1978. "Environmental Defense I: Introduction to Interest Group Advocacy in Complex Disputes." In *Public Interest Law: An Economic and Institutional Analysis*, ed. Burton Weisbrod. Berkeley: Univ. of California Press.

Truman, David B. 1951, 1971. *The Governmental Process.* New York: Knopf.

Twiss, Benjamin R. 1942. *Lawyers and the Constitution – How Laissez Faire Came to the Supreme Court.* Westport, Conn.: Greenwood.

U.S. News & World Report (23 April 1979). "Will Dissension Slow 'Right to Work' Drive?" 86:93–94.

———. (19 January 1976). "Behind the Storm Over Ford's Veto of Union 'Picketing' Bill." 80:74–75.

Victims Assistance Legal Organization. 1980–81. *A Report. 1980–1981: A Period of Transition.*

Viguerie, Richard E. 1981. *The New Right: We're Ready to Lead.* Falls Church, Va.: The Viguerie Co.

Vose, Clement E. 1955. "NAACP Strategy in the Restrictive Covenant Cases." *Western Reserve Law Review* 6:101–45.

———. 1957. "National Consumers' League and the Brandeis Brief." *Midwest Journal of Political Science* 1:178–90.

———. 1958. "Litigation as a Form of Pressure Group Activity." *Annals of the American Academy of Political and Social Science* 319:20–31.

———. 1959. *Caucasians Only.* Berkeley: Univ. of California Press.

———. 1966. "Interest Groups, Judicial Review, and Local Government." *Western Political Quarterly* 19:85–100.

———. 1972. *Constitutional Change.* Lexington, Mass.: Lexington.

———. 1981. "Interest Groups and Litigation." Paper presented to the American Political Science Association, New York.

Wall Street Journal (2 December 1975). "High Court to Decide If Chicago Suburb Can Be Racially Mixed," 6:2.

———— (30 December 1975). "Abusing the Spirit of the Law," 8:1.

———— (22 December 1976). "Group Alleges AFL-CIO Violated Election Law," 13:4.

———— (13 September 1977). "Union Shop Foes Split in Debate over Their Proper Role," 1:5.

———— (23 March 1977). "Trade Groups Fight Curbs on Raising Political Funds," 3:2.

Wasby, Stephen L. 1983. "Interest Group Litigation in an Age of Complexity." In *Interest Group Politics*, ed. Allen Cigler and Burdett Loomis. Washington, D.C., Congressional Quarterly.

Washington Legal Foundation. 1981. *Annual Report – 1981.*

————. 1982a. *Annual Report – 1982.*

————. 1982b. *Court Watch Manual: A Citizen's Guide to Accountability.*

Weinstein, Jack B. 1980. "Litigation Seeking Changes in Public Behavior and Institutions: Some Views on Participation." *University of California, Davis Law Review* 13:231–45.

Weisbrod, Burton A., ed. 1978. *Public Interest Law: An Economic and Institutional Analysis.* Berkeley: Univ. of California Press.

Wennberg, S. A. 1951. *Chamber of Commerce Administration.* Chicago, Ill.: National Institute for Commercial and Trade Organization Executives.

Wermeil, Stephen (23 April 1982). "Business Starts Pushing More at High Court." *Wall Street Journal*, p. 2.

Westin, Alan, 1962. "The Miracle Case: The Supreme Court and the Movies." In *Case Studies in American Government*, ed. Edwin A. Bock and Alan K. Campbell. Englewood Cliffs, N.J.: Prentice-Hall.

————. 1975. "Someone Has to Translate Rights into Realities." *Civil Liberties Review* 2:104–28.

Whitney, Glenna. (30 September 1982). "Ralph Nader of the Right to Open Office in Dallas." Reprinted by the Washington Legal Foundation from *Dallas Morning News.*

Wieder, Laurie C. 1982. Director of Communications, National Chamber Litigation Center. Interview with author.

Wilkins, Roy. 1955. "The Role of the NAACP in the Desegregation Process." *Social Problems* 2:201–4.

Wolfskill, George. 1962. *The Revolt of the Conservatives – A History of the American Liberty League.* Boston: Houghton Mifflin.

Wood, Jim. (12 July 1981). "Law Firm Fights for the Public's Other Side." Reprinted by the Washington Legal Foundation from *San Francisco Examiner.*

Wood, Stephen B. 1968. *Constitutional Politics in the Progressive Era – Child Labor and the Law.* Chicago: Univ. of Chicago Press.

Wood, Walter. (January 1920). "Official Letter to the Members of the League for Industrial Rights." *Law and Labor* 2.

Woodward, Bob, and Scott Armstrong. 1979. *The Brethren.* New York: Simon and Schuster.

Wootton, Graham. 1970. *Interest Groups.* Englewood Cliffs, N.J.: Prentice-Hall.

Yale Law Journal. 1949. "Private Attorneys-General: Action in the Fight for Civil Liberties." 58:574–98.

Zeigler, L. Harmon, and G. Wayne Peak. 1972. *Interest Groups in American Society.* Englewood Cliffs, N.J.: Prentice-Hall.

INDEX

economic groups (*cont.*)
   Advisory Council, Executive
   Committee of Southern Cot-
   ton Manufacturers, National
   Chamber Litigation Center,
   National Electric Light Asso-
   ciation, National Right to
   Work Committee, National
   Right to Work Legal Defense
   Foundation
Eddings v. Oklahoma, 132
Edison Electric Institute, 18, 28–
   30, 33, 45, 71; failure of, 30,
   38; litigation efforts, 28–30;
   origins, 28–29; publicity, 42;
   use of expert attorneys, 29,
   71
Eichelberger, J.S., 32
*Ellis v. Brotherhood of Railway
   and Airline Clerks,* 51
Ely, Joseph, 39
Emery, James, 24
Emory University, 160
employer associations: avoidance
   of litigation, 19, 25; litigation
   for, 16–24; and the National
   Consumers' League, 6–7; resort to the courts, 7
environmental impact statements,
   123
environmental law, 145, 157
Equal Employment Advisory
   Council, 45, 62–66, 91, 155,
   160; assessment of success,
   75–79; comparable worth
   litigation, 66; cooperation
   with other groups, 66; goals,
   64; litigation resources, 69–
   75, 143; origins, 63–64; resort
   to the courts, 67–68; strategy,
   64, 69, 149
Executive Committee of Southern
   Cotton Manufacturers, 18, 24–
   27, 34, 37, 45, 158; origins,
   24–25; planning litigation,
   26–27; use of litigation, 25

expert attorneys: and the Anti-
   Boycott Association, 22; anti-
   progressives, 39; conclusions
   on, 152–54; and conservative
   public interest law firms,
   140–41; and economic
   groups, 72–74; and the Edison Electric Institute, 29, 73;
   and the National Lawyers'
   Committee, 22; and the National Right to Work Legal
   Defense Foundation, 49; and
   the Pacific Legal Foundation,
   124; social groups, 110–13,
   117; and the Washington Legal Foundation, 132–33

Fair Labor Standards Act, 37
Fairchild, Charles S., 32, 34
Fairchild v. Colby, 33
Federal Child Labor Act: con-
   gressional battle over, 24; liti-
   gation battle over, 27; *see
   also Hammer v. Dagenhart*
Federal Commission on Obscenity
   and Pornography, 85, 108,
   113
Federal Election Commission, 53,
   69, 160
*FEC v. National Right to Work
   Committee,* 55
Federal Election Commission Act,
   62, 160
Federal Power Commission, 29,
   49
Federal Register, 60
Federal Trade Commission, 29,
   158
*First National Maintenance Cor-
   poration v. NLRB,* 61
Flast v. Cohen, 36
Flynt, Larry, 87
Flynt v. Ohio, 87
Ford Foundation, 150
Frankfurter, Felix, 157
free speech, 157